WORLD OF
BASEBALL

The Old
Ball Game

Mark Alvarez

A
REDEFINITION
BOOK

The Old Ball Game

Our Game

When I was in grammar school, I used to spend lunchtime and recess playing softball. It wasn't a formal game —not slow-pitch or fast-pitch or some other "official" version. It was just playground softball—no uniforms, no gloves. Just a bat and a rubber-covered ball about the size of a grapefruit. There was little strategy in our game. The pitcher tossed the ball in there for the batter to hit—no speed, no curves, no rainbow arch. When the batter took a pitch or swung and missed, the catcher caught the ball on the bounce and lobbed it back. We had no umpire, so there were no called balls and strikes. Batters swung when they felt like swinging, and social pressure was all we had to keep the game moving. When it *did* move, nothing we did was slick. Grounders bounced like frightened rabbits on the lumpy field, a lot of us just ducked hard line drives and every fly ball was a palm-stinging, finger-stubbing challenge. I didn't know it when I was ten, but I was playing a game remarkably close to the earliest kind of true American baseball: the so-called New York game popularized in the late 1840s by young Wall Street workers after office hours.

It wouldn't take much for those old-time baseball pioneers to feel right at home on our playgrounds. First, swap that grapefruit for a cheap hardball. Second, move the bases to about 30 yards apart. This distance, still standard, was part of the game's first written rules. Leave the pitcher alone. It took almost 50 years to nudge this central character back to the current 60 feet 6 inches. For now, the toss still comes in underhand from 45 feet or so away.

There are a few things we'd need to get used to if we actually took the field against those old New Yorkers. A foul ball doesn't count as a strike. A grounder that goes foul before it reaches first or third is playable. And

to make things a little easier on those sore hands—a hit caught on one bounce is an out, just like a ball caught on the fly. Oh, yes—one more thing: we'll play to 21 runs, rather than for six or seven or nine innings.

We should add an umpire too, even though there are no balls or strikes to call. He stands or sits off to the side and intrudes only when a decision isn't obvious. He also fines any players resorting to profanity—sometimes as much as a quarter.

We'll play just for fun, of course, not for money. A few friends or relatives might turn up to watch the game, but the idea of anyone *paying* for the privilege is ludicrous. Most playground veterans would be pretty comfortable with early baseball, and those old New York fellows would feel the same out behind the schoolhouse.

Of course, almost from the start, the sport began to change. Indeed, you could say that it was changing even *before* the start, because the New York game was just an improvement on other bat-and-ball games. Before long, members of athletic clubs started wearing uniforms; by 1849 the Knickerbockers were fitted out in white flannel shirts and blue trousers. By the late 1850s, a baseball association was formed—Americans love to organize. By 1860 or so, pitchers began to "cheat," throwing with a snap of the wrist and humming the ball in there with pinpoint control. Soon enough, spectators proved willing to pay to watch their favorite players perform.

This is the forgotten era of baseball —before elaborate rules and techniques, before press coverage and gambling and salary disputes, before baseball jargon was part of our language, before America had a national pastime. And it all started with a few young men out to play. Just like us.

Ballfields don't always mean dirt and grass. In a tenement alley around 1907, photographer Lewis Wickes Hines came upon this diamond in the rough.

By the late 1860s, the child's game that was to
become a nation's passion was growing up.
Soon it would become a window into America's
soul. "Whoever wants to know the heart and
mind of America had better learn baseball,"
wrote scholar Jacques Barzun.

Common Ancestors

PLAYING BALL

This 1820 woodcut is one of the earliest known representations of a game that might have been baseball, and appeared in a book entitled Children's Amusements. *During the same period, similar bat-and-ball games were enjoying increased popularity with boys in England and France as well.*

Americans have played ball for a lot longer than many of us think. In late 1621 the ship *Fortune* sailed into Plymouth harbor with 35 new immigrants to join the struggling year-old Massachusetts colony. Among them were a number of "lusty yonge men, and wilde enough." Puritans didn't celebrate Christmas as a holiday, so on December 25 of that year, most of the settlers, including Governor William Bradford, went off to their usual labor in field and forest. The robust newcomers, however, declared that they couldn't work on the day of their Savior's birth, so the elders gave the young men special permission to stay behind.

When the toiling colonists trudged home at midday, however, they found the new men, not reverently observing a holy day, but *playing ball*. Governor Bradford angrily put an end to this game by reprimanding the players and confiscating the ball.

The game these wilde yonge men were playing was stoolball, an old English pastime. And playing it on Christmas—even though it infuriated the Pilgrim fathers—was not unusual. From the earliest days of recorded history, ballgames have been associated with religious observances—a concept that many frenzied denizens of Fenway Park or Wrigley Field would have little trouble grasping today.

On the east wall of the Shrine of Hathor at the Temple of Deir-er-Bahari in Egypt is a 3,500-year-old painting; in it is what looks like an eccentric baseball coach hitting fly balls to his outfielders with a badly warped bat. In fact, it is Pharaoh Thothmes III hitting balls to a pair of priests. Thothmes wasn't just giving his local sandlot team a workout. Historians claim that such ancient ballgames were sacred rites. The ball embodied the idea of fertility, and ritual

ı la mort abatu lame li eftuet rendre
A ses vaches garder ne porra mes entendre

hitting, catching and throwing encouraged the annual spring rains to return to the parched land and the crops to grow once more along the Nile—concepts that put a whole new light on Opening Day.

In 15th-century England, ballgames were often played to celebrate religious holidays. Churchyards served as ballfields, and clergymen played alongside the yonge and wilde in their congregations at Easter. The game they commonly played was stoolball.

Stoolball was so called because stools were used as bases. One player stood in front of a stool and used his hand to swat the ball, while the thrower tried to slip it by him and bounce it off the little seat. They kept score by counting the number of times the hitter swatted the ball, and when the thrower hit his target, hitter and thrower changed places. With more players and more furniture, players ran from stool to stool after a hit and they were put out if a fielder drilled them with the ball before they could reach their goal.

Any modern American seeing this game in progress would recognize its resemblance—however distant—to baseball. And even if he didn't know that stools were once called "crickets," any modern Englishman, Australian or West Indian would notice that the upturned three-legged stool resembles the wicket that the batsman guards in cricket. Depending on how the stools were set up, stoolball players would have created a primitive cricket pitch or baseball diamond. Stoolball seems to be what anthropologists call a "common ancestor"—the primitive precursor of two great international sports.

The first known mention of baseball in print was not favorable. In 1700 a Puritan minister in England, the Reverend Mr. Thomas Wilson, sorrowfully

A monk's life in 14th-century France wasn't all prayer and deprivation. Fun and games for these monks in 1344 involved a bat, a ball and what appear to be outfielders.

The batting stance apparently goes back a lot further than most people think. This figure from ancient Mexico—made from clay and representing a warrior—dates from sometime between 200 and 600 A.D.

In 1744 a bat-and-ball game resembling baseball found its way into The Little Pretty Pocket Book, *a popular series of children's books in England. The woodcut was accompanied by the following rhyme:*

> *The Ball once struck off,*
> *Away flies the Boy*
> *To the next destin'd Post,*
> *And then Home with Joy.*

confessed that in his younger days he had seen "baseball and cricketts" played on the Sabbath. His sentiment remained common decades after baseball became our national pastime. In its early days, the National League allowed no Sunday baseball. During the first 16 years of this century, the great New York Giant pitcher Christy Mathewson refused to play on the Lord's Day, honoring a promise he'd made to his mother. He broke that promise in 1917, and got his just deserts when he was arrested for managing the Cincinnati Reds in a Sunday contest against the New York Giants. Later in the century, the Los Angeles Dodgers' Sandy Koufax was even stricter in observing the Jewish Sabbath and High Holy Days.

During the 18th century, both cricket and its baseball-like cousins were commonly played in England. In 1744 a children's book called *The Little Pretty Pocket Book* was published in London. It included an illustration of a "pitcher," a "runner" standing near a post that served as a base and a "batter" ready to hit the ball with his bare hand, as in the old game of stoolball.

Four years later, Mary Lepell, a royal maid of honor, wrote that the family of the Prince of Wales "[divert] themselves at base-ball, a play all who are or have been schoolboys are well acquainted with." And at the end of the century, Jane Austen listed the game with other youthful diversions in her novel *Northanger Abbey,* writing that Catherine preferred "cricket, base ball, riding on horseback, and running about the country . . . to books."

Cricket and baseball had begun to meander down their separate paths late in the 17th century. Cricket adopted a standard set of rules much sooner, while "baseball" remained a primitive pastime—played under different names

INN	TEAM	1G	2G	INN	TEAM	1G	2G
	L.A.	7	0	8	BALT	3	0
1	CHI	5	1		BOS	4	2
2	N.Y.	5	0		K.C.	
	DET	4	0		MINN	TN-2
7	WASH	3	8			
	CLEV	15	4			

with different rules in different locations—well into the 19th century. One common version was known as "rounders," in which four posts served as bases, batters ran clockwise—in the opposite direction from modern baseball—and a runner could be put out by being hit with the ball. Running all four bases successfully was, of course, a "rounder." Rounders is still a school sport in England, played using a one-handed bat, a leather-covered ball, upright posts as bases and no gloves.

British soldiers played cricket in New York City during the War of Independence, and cricket clubs existed in cities throughout the original 13 colonies. At the same time, American farmers and townspeople, without the time to perfect the sophisticated skills required for cricket, played what was variously known as "round ball," "town ball," "goal ball" or "base ball"—usually putting the ball into play with a bat rather than their bare hands.

In April 1778 at Valley Forge, a Revolutionary soldier named George Ewing wrote in his journal that he "exercisd in the afternoon in the intervals playd base"—the first written reference to the game in America. Imagine how happy the soldiers who had spent the vicious winter at Valley Forge must have been to see "base" season roll around.

During the next decade, "baste ball" was a popular sport at Princeton College, where it was "much practised by the smaller boys among the students and by the grammar Scholars with balls and sticks in the back common." The game was banned by the administration because it "is in itself low and unbecoming gentlemen Students, and . . . is an exercise attended with great danger." Ballplaying in the streets of Worcester, Massachusetts, was also banned by ordinance in 1816.

Refusing to play on religious holidays and the Sabbath is a time-honored baseball tradition, updated in the dead-ball era by Giant pitcher Christy Mathewson, who refused to play on Sundays, and later by Dodger pitcher Sandy Koufax (above), who opted out of Game 1 of the 1965 World Series because it fell on the Jewish high holy day of Yom Kippur.

In 1834 Boston Common—not Fenway Park—was the hub of baseball in the city. This woodcut appeared in Robin Carver's The Book of Sports *with a description of the game of base ball that was virtually identical to the game of rounders.*

- A GAME AT BASE BALL.

But sensible authorities couldn't dampen the popularity of these simple ball-and-stick games that youngsters all over the country enjoyed. And youngsters weren't the only ones to take part; adults, too, played ball when workingmen with a little free time on their hands could get together. Some suggest that the term "town ball" resulted from the game's being played on New England greens and commons on town meeting day, when Yankees took time off from their normal pursuits to combine self-government with self-amusement.

During the first decades of the 1800s, young men with a bit of leisure time began to play ball together regularly for fun and exercise. Thurlow Weed, the notorious New York state political boss, remembered that he had belonged to a baseball club in Rochester in 1825 and that the club had nearly 50 members, aged 18 to 40. Town ball, like "baste ball," was popular among college students. A Brown University student named Williams Latham wrote in 1827: "We this morning have been playing ball. . . . But I never have received so much pleasure from it here as I have in Bridgewater. They do not have more than 6 or 7 on a side, so that a great deal of time is spent in running after the ball."

In 1829 a volume entitled *The Boy's Own Book* was published in London, and it contained a set of rules for playing rounders, among other games. In 1834 an imitator, *The Book of Sports,* was issued in Boston. It contained virtually the same rules for rounders, but the publishers changed the heading to "Base, or Goal Ball" to reflect American terminology. Accompanying the rules was a woodcut of the game being played by youngsters on Boston Common—the first illustration of baseball being played in this

country. The players in the woodcut are using the common's intersecting paths as part of their diamond, and historian Robert Henderson suggests that this custom led to the idea of cutting away the turf on a baseball diamond to leave dirt basepaths.

Town ball was also known as the Massachusetts game and as such was pretty popular on Boston Common in the late 1860s (above). It featured batting lineups of 10 to 14 players, three strikes for an out and four-foot stakes as bases. Whoever scored 100 tallies first was the winner.

For the most part, rounders and primitive American baseball were the same game. But while the various rounders-like games shared several common elements, rules were anything but standard. There are accounts of as many as 50 players involved in some games. Posts were still in general use as bases, though flat stones were common, too. Balls —usually made of rags with stitched leather covers—were quite soft. That was a good thing, because all of the games still relied on hitting the runner with a thrown ball—"soaking" or "burning"—to put him out. In some games, three missed swings put the striker out. In most, a ball caught on the fly was an out. In some, so were balls caught on a single hop. No one wore a glove, of course.

Despite baseball's popularity among college students and young men in general, baseball was still thought of as a children's game, and there was a real prejudice against grown men wasting time with it. Nevertheless, a few grown-ups persisted. Tom Heitz of the National Baseball Library thinks that this prejudice against men playing children's games was partly overcome by the country's first "health kick." Serious epidemics such as malaria and typhoid fever in growing cities encouraged physicians to recommend vigorous outdoor activity as a way to maintain good health. In 1833 the Olympic Town Ball Club of Philadelphia was formed—the first American club to last any significant length of time. The Olympics played

With only one out to an inning in town ball, getting soaked—being put out by being hit with the ball, as demonstrated above in a modern re-creation—was an instant rally killer.

town ball until 1860—long after most of the country had converted to real baseball.

Although the Olympics were formed in Pennsylvania, town ball was really a New England game; in fact, it came to be called "the Massachusetts game" to distinguish it from "the New York game" favored on Manhattan Island. Like all the other bat-and-ball games, it was similar to rounders, but it had its own distinct rules and playing field. In the Massachusetts game, the basepaths formed a square, with posts for bases. The four posts were 60 feet apart, and players ran counterclockwise from one to the next. The batter, or "striker," stood not at one of the corner points, but at a "stand" halfway between the first post and the fourth. The "feeder" threw overhand from 30 feet away. There were no balls or strikes, so his job was simply to lay the ball in there to be hit. Once the striker put the ball into play, he ran from post to post, but didn't return to his hitting position to score: he did that by reaching the fourth post before a fielder hit him with the ball. There was no concept of force plays or tagging up after a fly, or even of runners having to stay within the baseline between posts. They could, and often did, take off for the outfield with the fielding team in hot pursuit—anything to avoid being "soaked." As in cricket, there was no foul territory, and some teams became adept at the "back game," in which they purposely hit the ball behind them. To guard against this, fielding teams sometimes stationed three or four defenders behind the striker's stand.

Town ball in the Bay State was a sort of false start on the road to baseball. It was an advance on the primitive, loosely structured bat-and-ball games played around the country, and it might eventually have caught on in

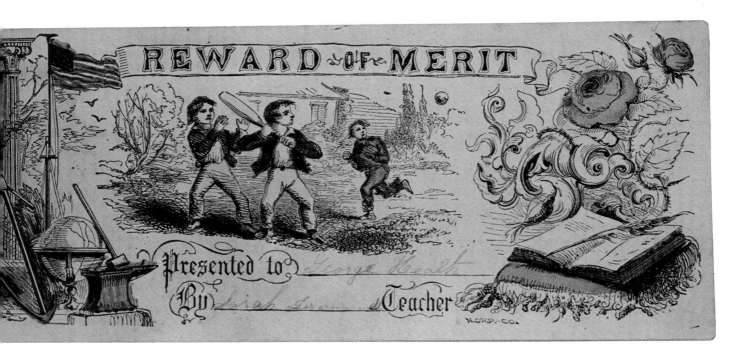

other regions as more and more young men looked for ways to spend their leisure time. But it took until 1858 for an association to establish a set of official town ball rules. The next year the first intercollegiate ballgame was played by those Massachusetts rules, Amherst besting Williams, 73–32.

But another game had already come along, relegating town ball to the bat rack of history. In the early 1840s a group of young Manhattanites organized an athletic club, and one of their members suggested writing up a set of rules for a bat-and-ball game that they played among themselves. The bases were about 90 feet apart. "Soaking" the runner was abandoned in favor of the more gentlemanly tag. Three strikes meant the batter was out, though he could run to first if the catcher dropped the final strike. Innings, in which "three hands out, all out," determined the number of chances a team had to bat. And although this game had definite rules, it had infinite possibilities. A game that began as a private amusement grew into the New York game, and within a quarter-century, became our national pastime. It was baseball. Real baseball. ◉

The concept of the scholar-athlete apparently dates back as far as 1845, when certificates for scholastic achievement carried images of ballplayers on them.

The Name of the Game

Baseball jargon is as old as the sport itself. Here are some terms and definitions from the game's early days; most are no longer in use. The cartoons are from William Crane's *A Comprehensive View of Baseball,* 1859, and the *New York Graphic,* 1874.

Aces: Runs.

Ash: A bat, since bats are usually made from white ash.

Blinder: A shutout.

Bounder: A bouncing ball that does not go out of the infield.

Burning, plugging, plunking or **soaking:** Putting a player out by hitting him with the ball.

An "eye-deal" decision.

Chicago or **skunk:** To shut out an opponent.

Cranks: Baseball fans.

Daisy cutter: A sharply hit ground ball.

Catching a "daisy cutter."

Fair-foul hit: A hit that falls in fair territory, then bounces foul between home and the base (playable until 1877).

Feeder: The pitcher in rounders.

First nine: The best players on an amateur ballclub. Some clubs also had second, third and muffin nines.

Foul bound: A foul ball caught after one bounce for an out.

Foul fly: A pop foul, specifically one that is caught for an out.

Catching a ball "on the fly."

Hand: A player. When a player is out, a hand is lost.

Kicking: Arguing with the umpire over a call.

Match or **match game:** A game between two clubs, as opposed to intraclub games.

Muffin: A muffed ball is a missed catch or grounder; a muffin is the least talented player on the team. Also called a "scrub."

A "cat-cher" playing "muffins."

Over-pitch: A wild pitch.

Pecker: The pitcher in rounders.

Picked nine: An early type of all-star team; the best local players from a number of clubs chosen to play a specific team passing through the area.

Revolver: A player who breaks a contractual obligation in order to play with another team.

Rigs: Baseball uniforms.

Rubber game: The third game when two teams have split the first two games.

Safety: A safe hit.

Short field: An early name for the shortstop.

Striker: An old term for the batter, dating back to rounders.

A "Miss" by the batter, beautifully caught.

Tally: To score a run.

Treble play: A triple play.

Wide: A called ball.

Modern baseball is the product of a long evolution. Early stick-and-ball games like stoolball and one old cat needed only a few players and a minimum of equipment. Rules were simple and could easily be adapted to the number of players or limits of a field.

The sophisticated game of cricket was played in Britain and its colonies in the 18th and 19th centuries, largely by the upper classes. The simpler schoolyard game of rounders, which is still played in England, broke off i two games on this side of the Atlantic: town ball, or the Massachusetts ga and the New York game of baseball.

The New York game's popularity surged in the 1850s, displacing both to ball and cricket. It was played widely by troops during the Civil War, and by 1870s baseball had become the United States' first truly national sp

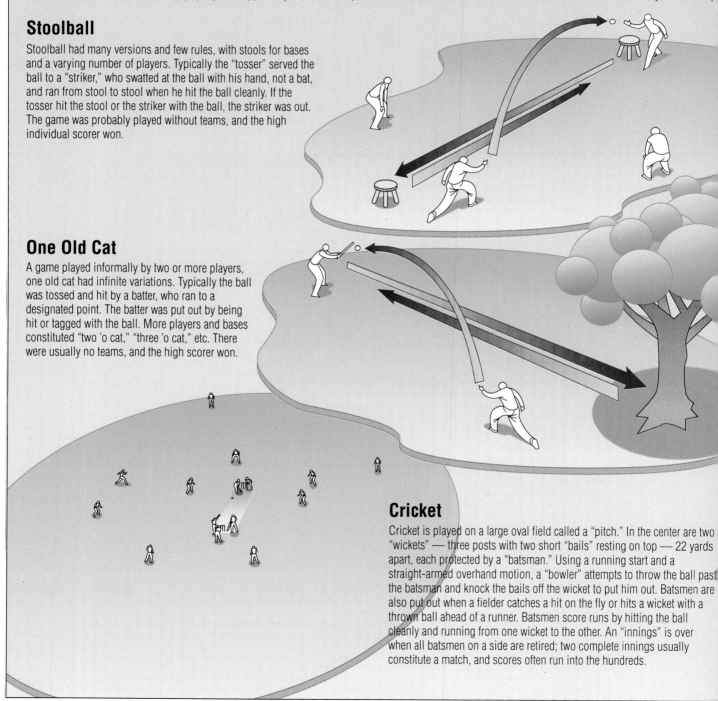

Stoolball

Stoolball had many versions and few rules, with stools for bases and a varying number of players. Typically the "tosser" served the ball to a "striker," who swatted at the ball with his hand, not a bat, and ran from stool to stool when he hit the ball cleanly. If the tosser hit the stool or the striker with the ball, the striker was out. The game was probably played without teams, and the high individual scorer won.

One Old Cat

A game played informally by two or more players, one old cat had infinite variations. Typically the ball was tossed and hit by a batter, who ran to a designated point. The batter was put out by being hit or tagged with the ball. More players and bases constituted "two 'o cat," "three 'o cat," etc. There were usually no teams, and the high scorer won.

Cricket

Cricket is played on a large oval field called a "pitch." In the center are two "wickets" — three posts with two short "bails" resting on top — 22 yards apart, each protected by a "batsman." Using a running start and a straight-armed overhand motion, a "bowler" attempts to throw the ball past the batsman and knock the bails off the wicket to put him out. Batsmen are also put out when a fielder catches a hit on the fly or hits a wicket with a thrown ball ahead of a runner. Batsmen score runs by hitting the ball cleanly and running from one wicket to the other. An "innings" is over when all batsmen on a side are retired; two complete innings usually constitute a match, and scores often run into the hundreds.

Rounders

Rounders, another old English game, used posts for bases, with the goal to one side of the batting square. Today a nine-person team is normal, although in the 19th century teams sometimes had more players. A bowler pitches underhand to a batsman, who swings a short bat with one hand. As in cricket, the batsman runs with bat in hand, and as long as a runner touches the pole with hand or bat he or she cannot be tagged out. A runner reaching the fourth post scores a "rounder." Once a batsman is out, he or she cannot bat again in the innings; the innings is over when the entire side is out. The team with the most runs after two innings wins.

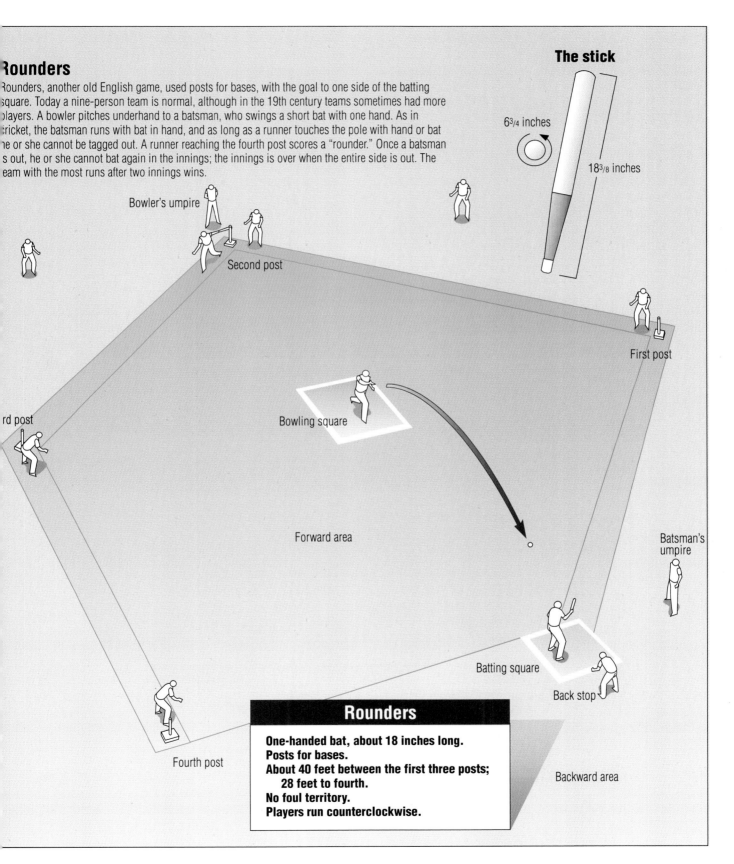

The stick

6³/₄ inches

18³/₈ inches

Bowler's umpire

Second post

rd post

Bowling square

Forward area

First post

Batsman's umpire

Batting square

Back stop

Fourth post

Backward area

Rounders

One-handed bat, about 18 inches long.
Posts for bases.
About 40 feet between the first three posts;
**   28 feet to fourth.**
No foul territory.
Players run counterclockwise.

Town Ball (The Massachusetts Game)

Popular throughout New England, New York state and Pennsylvania, town ball was played by two teams to a fixed number of "tallies." Bases were stakes set in a square about 60 feet apart and were run clockwise or counterclockwise. The "striker" stood midway between the "first stake" and "home bound." The "thrower" stood 35 feet away and threw the ball overhand. An out was made by a batter swinging and missing three times, a fielder catching a batted ball the fly, or a runner being "plugged" by a thrown ball. The Massachusetts Association of Base Ball Players adopted rules in 1858 calling for bases 6 feet apart, 10 to 14 players per side, one out per side to an inning and 10 tallies to win a "match game."

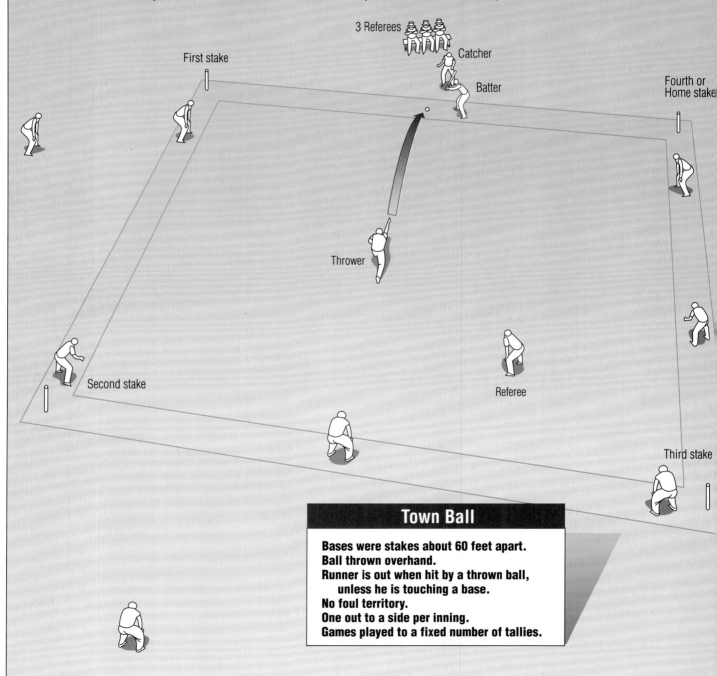

3 Referees

Catcher

Batter

First stake

Fourth or
Home stake

Thrower

Second stake

Referee

Third stake

Town Ball

Bases were stakes about 60 feet apart.
Ball thrown overhand.
Runner is out when hit by a thrown ball,
   unless he is touching a base.
No foul territory.
One out to a side per inning.
Games played to a fixed number of tallies.

aseball (The New York Game)

and around New York City, the game took a different shape, and rules
wn up by the Knickerbocker Club in 1845 became widely accepted as
ndard. The distance between bases was 90 feet, and the "striker's point"
d "home base" were the same. The ball was pitched underhand from a
cher's box, not a mound, 45 feet from the striker. Batted balls landing
tside the first- or third-baselines were not playable. Runners could be

tagged out or forced out at the base. Hits could be caught on the fly or on a
single bounce for an out, but by 1858 only on the fly. Teams generally had
9 players — rarely more than 11 — and each team had 3 outs to an inning.
Games were originally played to 21 "aces," or runs, but eventually nine
players and nine innings became standard. Except for changes in pitching,
modern baseball uses the same basic rules.

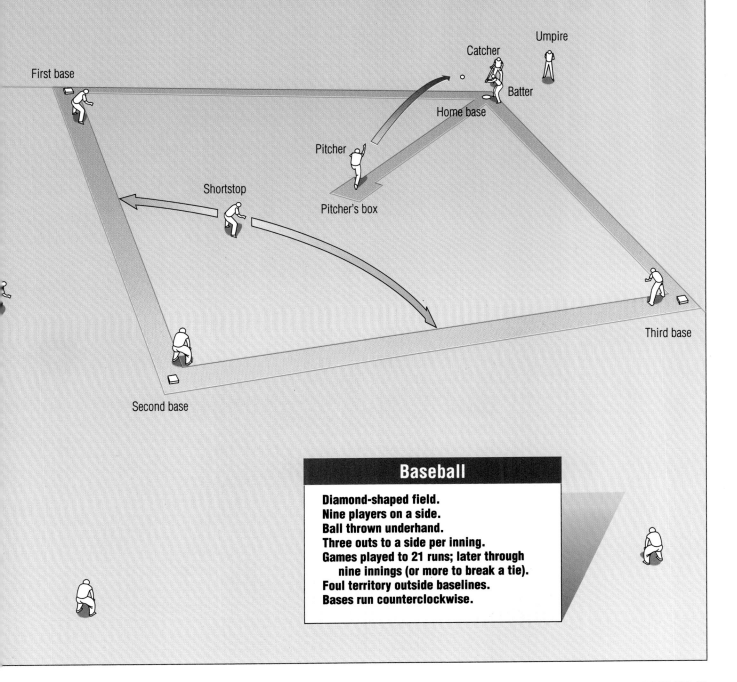

Umpire

Catcher

First base

Batter

Home base

Pitcher

Pitcher's box

Shortstop

Third base

Second base

Baseball

Diamond-shaped field.
Nine players on a side.
Ball thrown underhand.
Three outs to a side per inning.
Games played to 21 runs; later through
nine innings (or more to break a tie).
Foul territory outside baselines.
Bases run counterclockwise.

The Doubleday Myth

Major General Abner Doubleday won posthumous acclaim for supposedly inventing baseball in Cooperstown, New York, in 1839. But Doubleday should rightly have been more famous for his role in the battles of Fort Sumter and Gettysburg. According to historian Harold Peterson, "Abner Doubleday didn't invent baseball. Baseball invented Abner Doubleday."

The Civil War helped pass the emerging game of baseball to the south and west, as Union soldiers (preceding page) brought the tools of the game along with the tools of war. "For Union troops, baseball supplied a poignant reminder of home, especially on major holidays, when it took the place of family gatherings," wrote Joel Zoss and John Bowman in Diamonds in the Rough.

Millions of Americans who know almost nothing about baseball know that the game was invented by a fellow named Abner Doubleday. Even though it wasn't. And even casual fans know that the Baseball Hall of Fame is in Cooperstown, New York, because that's where Doubleday created the national pastime. Even though it's not. It is certain that Abner Doubleday did *not* invent the sport of baseball. To believe the Doubleday myth today is to believe in a flat earth. But the fable—cooked up for purely commercial reasons by a committee more than 80 years ago—has taken on a life of its own. Why and how did this West Point graduate and Civil War general come to be credited with inventing baseball?

In April 1889 a group of American baseball players sailed into New York harbor on the steamship *Adriatic*. They were returning from England, the last stop on Albert Goodwill Spalding's much-ballyhooed world tour. One of the game's great pitchers before and during the National Association era, Spalding had since helped establish the National League, had become president of the Chicago White Stockings and had founded the A.G. Spalding & Bros. sporting goods company. The real reason for the tour was to popularize the game of baseball in Australia and Europe so that Spalding could tap into new markets for his equipment. But Spalding, who understood publicity and public relations as well as any man alive, knew that his bread and butter remained in the United States; he wasn't about to let his returning heroes pass quietly through the country's biggest city.

So a banquet was organized for the ballplayers, to be held at the fashionable Delmonico's Restaurant on the corner of 26th and Broadway. The

HEAD QUARTERS, 76TH REGT N.Y.S.V.
CAMP DOUBLEDAY,
Lieut Col. John D. Shaul, commanding.

restaurant walls were decorated with enlarged photographs of the players in exotic locations around the globe, and more than 300 people turned out in their honor. The evening was also a time, as public address announcers say before the National Anthem, to honor America. The players weren't just welcomed home; they were praised as "gladiators . . . covered with their American manhood."

The all-male event was hosted by A. G. Mills, president of the National League, and was attended by such luminaries as Teddy Roosevelt and popular writer and humorist Mark Twain. By all accounts, it was a sparkling and boisterous affair. The banquet was "served in nine innings," seasoned by the renowned actor DeWolf Hopper reciting "Casey at the Bat" and peppered with speeches and humorous toasts. Twain, toasting the Sandwich Islands —a stop on the tour—delivered a famous, if not entirely serious, address, calling baseball "the very symbol, the outward and visible expression of the drive and push and rush and struggle of the raging, tearing, booming nineteenth century."

Between toasts, President Mills took the podium and did a little raging and booming himself. In a burst of patriotism spurred on by champagne and cigars, he asserted the purely American lineage of baseball. This was music to the ears of those present; Americans naturally wanted to believe that their national sport was entirely homegrown, and they could not accept that it had descended from an English children's game. Mills' exuberant companions took up the cry: "No rounders," they shouted joyfully, "no rounders! NO ROUNDERS!"

Mills rested his diatribe on a pamphlet written the year before by John Montgomery Ward entitled *Base Ball, How to Become a Player with the Ori-*

Because he fired the first shot in the defense of Fort Sumter, a skirmish that touched off the Civil War, Abner Doubleday had a Union Army camp (above) in Washington, D.C., named after him. That the soldiers there appeared to play some form of baseball is just a bizarre coincidence. As Branch Rickey once said, "The only thing General Doubleday ever started was the Civil War."

By the time he launched his campaign in 1905 to declare baseball a uniquely American sport, Al Spalding had held one of the game's highest profiles for almost 40 years. A player, manager, team owner and sporting goods manufacturer, Spalding was tireless in his promotion of the game. Sportswriter Henry Chadwick called him a "stirring Western merchant, full of nerve, pluck, independence and push."

gin, History, and Explanation of the Game. Ward was a veteran shortstop for the New York Giants, an attorney and president of the Brotherhood of Professional Base Ball Players, and he had written critically of "persons who believed that everything good and beautiful in the world must be of English origin." His pamphlet was an attempt to demonstrate that baseball was purely American. Many of his facts—and most of his conclusions—were simply wrong. But his history of the game told people like Mills what they wanted to hear. As a result, Ward's treatise served for decades as the basis of the case against rounders.

E ven the most chauvinistic proponents of New World baseball understood that the game didn't leap full-blown from the mind of some great frontier sportsman. Spalding himself was always quite willing to believe that baseball had evolved. But he followed Ward's spurious argument that it derived directly from the "American" game of one old cat rather than the "British" game of rounders.

In his pamphlet, Ward had attacked an unnamed—and unpatriotic—baseball writer for pushing the rounders theory. Everyone knew that he was talking about Henry Chadwick, the preeminent baseball journalist of the 19th century, who had seen his first baseball game in 1848, and to whom there was no question about baseball's debt to the English game. His position was simple: "Base Ball originated from the old English schoolboy game of Rounders, as plainly shown by the fact that the basic principle of both games is the field use of a bat, a ball and bases." Lacrosse, he said, was the only field game that had a strictly American origin, having been first played by American Indians.

By 1867 Americans were singing—and dancing—the praises of baseball, but it was still far from the game we know today. Basemen were literally that—they played their position standing on the base—and in this fanciful rendition the artist includes a second batter.

Chadwick and Spalding argued this question for years. Their disagreement was a friendly one, but it always had an edge to it. Chadwick was the editor of the annual *Spalding's Official Base Ball Guide* from 1881 to 1908. The position gave him great status in the baseball world and served as a bully pulpit, which he used to denounce everything from alcoholism to overreliance on the home run. But it also made him Spalding's employee. A.G. always treated "Father Chadwick" with respect, calling him "the Grand Old Man of Base Ball," complimenting him on "the magnificent work he has done in the upbuilding of the game." But there was no doubt about who the boss was.

Chadwick, old and increasingly frail, opened the 1903 *Base Ball Guide* with a survey of baseball's history as he saw it. "Just as the New York game was improved townball," he wrote, "so was townball an improved form of the two-centuries-old English game of rounders." Appearing in the authoritative *Spalding Guide,* this was likely to become the accepted point of view. Not at all what the proprietor had in mind.

Chadwick's essay was accurate, if oversimplified. But Spalding referred to it as "rounder pap" and refused "to swallow any more of it without some substantial proof sauce with it." Spalding had a personal motive in rejecting Chadwick's theory. He recalled touring England in 1874 with the Boston and Philadelphia National Association clubs, when sneering English spectators claimed, in his words, "Why it's nothing but our old game of Rounders, that we used to play with the gals when we were byes." The idea that his country's national sport—the game that supplied him with his livelihood and his business with its very existence—could be dismissed so easily moved Spalding to fury. He simply wouldn't stand for the suggestion that baseball had evolved from rounders, which he called "that asinine pastime."

OLD JUDGE CIGARETTES Goodwin & Co., New York.

As president of the Brotherhood of Baseball Players, John Montgomery Ward was the game's first player-labor leader. But in his pamphlet on the history of the game, he also provided management—namely Al Spalding and the Mills Commission—with an anthem for declaring baseball an American original.

Sportswriter Henry Chadwick, editor of Spalding's Base Ball Guide, *made the case for baseball having evolved from the British game of rounders, but was realistic enough to realize that Spalding had stacked the Mills Commission to render a more patriotic verdict, the facts notwithstanding. "The whole thing," Chadwick wrote, "was a joke between Albert and myself."*

In 1905 Spalding used his Base Ball Guide *as a public relations tool in his effort to convince the world that baseball originated in the U.S.A. He had long ago convinced fans that the* Guide *was an official league publication, when in fact it was not.*

So in 1905 Spalding himself led off the *Guide* with a six-page article provocatively titled:

What is the origin of
BASE BALL?
Did It Originate From
The English Game of
ROUNDERS
The Colonial Game of
ONE OLD CAT
The New England and
Philadelphia Game of
TOWN BALL
Or
WHAT?

In that piece, Spalding described the game of rounders he and his men had played when the world tour visited Liverpool, and he made rounders sound very silly indeed. Clearly, it wasn't a game for grown men of a serious athletic bent. He didn't bother to point out that this was the very reason Americans had tinkered with rounders for so many years, finally transforming it into the "New York game" of baseball.

The boss continued to attack his editor's theory by demonstrating all the ways in which baseball and rounders were different. At the end of his discourse, Spalding "requested" that James Sullivan, President of the American Sports Publishing Company, organize a formal investigation into the origin of

Continued on page 32

Made in Canada

It might make Al Spalding roll over in his grave, but the first baseball game may have been played in Canada. Just as baseball in the United States has its Abner Doubleday story, Canadian baseball has its own creation myth. And for Americans, the bad news is that the Canadian legend places the first ballgame in 1838, a full year before the young men of Cooperstown supposedly got together to try out Doubleday's new game.

In 1886 a physician named Adam Ford wrote a letter to *Sporting Life,* stating that he had been present on June 4, 1838, Militia Muster Day, when the first baseball game was played. He recalled clearly how, nearly 50 years before, a group of men from Zorra township in Ontario took on a team from Oxford township. Ford gave the names of all the players and included in his letter to the Philadelphia magazine a detailed diagram of the square ballfield that the men marked off in a pasture. According to him, the baselines were 21 yards long, the "thrower" stood 18 yards from the catcher, and there was fair and foul territory—or, as Ford said, "fair hits" and "no hits." The ball, fashioned by the local shoemaker, was made of yarn covered with calfskin, and the bats used were either cedar sticks or wagon wheel spokes.

Even though Ford didn't remember the score or who won the game, his memory of that day is nothing short of miraculous, especially considering that he was only seven years old when the alleged game took place. By the time he wrote the letter to *Sporting Life,* Dr. Ford was a 55-year-old alcoholic who had fled his native country after reportedly killing a man by administering a drug supposed to lessen the effects of drunkenness.

Even if Ford is not the most reliable of sources, the players that he named did exist. And if the game that Ontarians played that day was not exactly baseball, they were playing the game soon thereafter. And by the 1880s, Canada had its own professional teams, leagues and ballparks, not to mention the fact that it had exported some of its best athletes to the States: Bill Phillips, who played first base for Cleveland, as well as for Brooklyn and Kansas City in the American Association; Pop Smith, who played for six NL teams over 12 years; and the St. Louis Browns' Tip O'Neill, who won the Triple Crown in 1887.

True or not, Ford's story merely echoes what historians already know: that Canadians were playing baseball as early as their neighbors to the south. And many were playing it just as well.

baseball. He also nominated a "Special Board of Base Ball Commissioners" to study the material unearthed by Sullivan.

Besides being a publisher, James E. Sullivan was also president of the AAU—the Amateur Athletic Union. For years his was a strong voice in American sports, and his name lives on in the Sullivan Award, bestowed yearly on the best amateur athlete in the United States. But the American Sports Publishing Company was a Spalding-owned business, and Sullivan, like Chadwick, was a Spalding employee.

The members of the board—handpicked by Spalding—were respected figures. Morgan Bulkeley was a former governor and current U.S. senator from Connecticut—and the first president of the National League. Arthur Gorman, who died while the board was still in existence, was a former U.S. senator from Maryland. Nick Young was the fourth president of the National League and a longtime baseball functionary who owed his status to his friend Spalding. Al Reach and George Wright were both famous old-time ballplayers who had developed successful sporting goods businesses before selling them to—you guessed it—A.G. Spalding & Bros. Finally, the man who became the board's chairman was Abraham G. "No Rounders" Mills.

Over the next few years, Sullivan, as secretary of the Mills Commission, as the board came to be known, was "deluged" with a tidal wave of "letters and manuscripts . . . bearing upon the question of the origin of Base Ball." On a lark, Henry Chadwick submitted a "statement of incontrovertible facts," styling himself "Counsel for the Defense." But he was a poor advocate, providing nothing more than familiar, accurate information about the similarities between rounders and baseball. Chadwick failed to offer either historical evidence or a powerful argument to nail down his case. Spalding

Sliding wasn't recommended in town ball, as the "bases" were four-foot wooden stakes. Above, Tom Heitz, librarian at the National Baseball Hall of Fame Library and manager of the Cooperstown Leatherstockings, does the honors.

weighed in with a letter six times as long, a tirade similar to his article in the 1905 *Guide,* but with a difference: this time, he directed the commission's attention to a letter from Abner Graves, a mining engineer from Denver.

Born and raised in Cooperstown, New York, Graves claimed to have been there on the day in 1839 when Abner Doubleday had his revelation. According to Spalding, Graves wrote that Doubleday "outlined with a stick in the dirt the present diamond-shaped Base Ball field, indicating the location of the players in the field, and afterward [Graves] saw him make a diagram of the field on paper, with a crude pencil memorandum of the rules for his new game, which he named *Base Ball.*"

"I am very strongly inclined to the belief that Cooperstown, N.Y. is the birthplace of the present American game of Base Ball," Spalding wrote to the Mills Commission, "and that Major General Abner Doubleday was the originator of the game."

Mills and his commission took the hint. All of them understood that baseball was a business and, as such, had to be marketed and promoted. They knew that appealing to Americans' pride could be good for attendance, so they didn't let the facts get in their way.

Mills, who had also been a Civil War officer, had known Doubleday personally. They had been members of the same military veterans organization in New York, and upon Doubleday's death, Mills was in charge of the memorial service. Clearly, if the general had had any connection with baseball, Mills wouldn't have needed a letter from Colorado to inform him about it.

But that's just what he claimed in his report to Sullivan. "Until my perusal of this testimony," he wrote—almost certainly with tongue in cheek—"my own belief had been that our game of Base Ball . . . originated

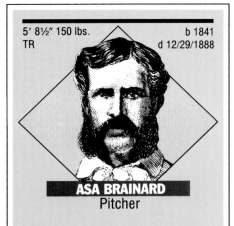

5' 8½" 150 lbs.
TR
b 1841
d 12/29/1888

ASA BRAINARD
Pitcher

What kind of pitching staff does it take for a baseball team to have an undefeated season? Well, in 1869 the Cincinnati Red Stockings did it with a staff of one: Asa Brainard. A heavy drinker and a clown, the former New York Knickerbocker was a smashing success in the box but a constant source of aggravation to his stern manager, Harry Wright. Once during a game, Brainard tried to plunk a rabbit that was running across the field, and two runs scored on his "wild pitch."

Brainard was a gifted athlete and one of the first to experiment with different deliveries and changes in pitching style. Instead of softly tossing the ball toward the batter, Brainard used speed—and a little snap. One early history, *Baseball in Cincinnati,* said, "He delivered a swift, twisting sort of ball. . . . He very rarely pitched the ball where the batsman expected it, but sent them in too high, too low, or too close to the striker, until the latter became nervous or irritated."

As other pitchers began duplicating his delivery and his heavy drinking took its toll, Brainard lost his edge. He played in the National Association from 1871 through 1874, but it was a downhill ride that culminated in his retirement after an atrocious 5–24 season with the Lord Baltimores in 1874.

Brainard moved west, eventually settling in Denver, where he ran a pool room.

Men of a New York state regiment brought their version of baseball with them to Fort Pulaski, Georgia, after capturing the fort from Confederate forces in November 1861. Almost everyone wore blue, except the pitcher (above, center), who wore white.

with the Knickerbocker club of New York, and it was frequently referred to as the 'New York Ball Game.' "

The Knickerbockers had been mentioned before by John Ward, by Chadwick, who had actually seen them play, and by Spalding, who noted in his 1905 article that it was the 60th anniversary of their founding. In fact, up until the time the Mills Commission issued its report, it was generally believed —on good evidence—that modern baseball had begun with improvements that these gentlemen had made on the primitive bat-and-ball games of the day. Ironically, the Knickerbockers probably would have served as well as Abner Doubleday to "prove" that baseball was distinctly American.

But the promoter in Spalding couldn't resist the public relations plum that Graves had handed him: "It certainly appeals to an American's pride," he wrote, "to have had the great national game of Base Ball created and named by a Major General in the United States Army, and to have that same game played as a camp diversion by the soldiers of the Civil War, who, at the conclusion of the war, disseminated Base Ball throughout the length and breadth of the United States, and thus gave to the game its national character."

The commission's final report, in the form of a letter by Mills to Sullivan, came to a crisp, unequivocal conclusion: "First: That 'Base Ball' had its origin in the United States. Second: That the first scheme for playing it, according to the best evidence obtainable to date, was devised by Abner Doubleday at Cooperstown, N.Y. in 1839."

Chadwick later called the Mills Commission report "a masterly piece of special pleading, which lets my dear old friend Albert escape a bad defeat." Nonetheless, Spalding was happy, and America was assured that its national

THE NATIONAL GAME. THREE "OUTS" AND ONE "RUN".
ABRAHAM WINNING THE BALL.

pastime had been invented by, in Spalding's words, "the man who sighted the first gun fired from Fort Sumter, April 12, 1861, which opened the War of the Rebellion between North and South."

But there were a few small problems with the Mills Commission's findings. First of all, Abner Doubleday wasn't in Cooperstown during the spring or summer of 1839. He was at the U.S. Military Academy at West Point, New York, learning to be a soldier. Second, during his lifetime—he died in 1893—Doubleday had never spoken of baseball outside of the instance recalled by Graves. Once, in describing his youth, the general replied that "I was fond of poetry and art and much interested in mathematical studies. In my outdoor sports, I was addicted to topographical work and even as a boy amused myself by making maps of the country around my father's residence." Not exactly the reply you'd expect from the proud father of the national pastime.

According to Tom Heitz, head of the National Baseball Library at the Hall of Fame, there *was* an Abner Doubleday living in Cooperstown in 1839—a young cousin of the Civil War officer. Heitz thinks that Abner Graves might have confused the two. But he says there's no reason to think that the younger Doubleday played anything but town ball. A close look at Graves' letter supports that position. The game he describes Doubleday inventing is a far cry from modern baseball.

The boys of Cooperstown were apparently playing a version of one old cat, similar to the game familiar even today as "scrub." Between 20 and 50 of the Otsego Academy and Green's Select School scholars participated at one time in these matches. The batter hit the ball, ran to a "goal" 50 feet away and

Baseball was an early metaphor for politics, as shown in this Currier & Ives lithograph that appeared shortly after the 1860 presidential election. Republican Abraham Lincoln (far right) was the winning pitcher, and the losers included, from left, John Bell of the Union Party, Stephen Douglas of the Northern Democrats and John C. Breckinridge of the Southern Democrats.

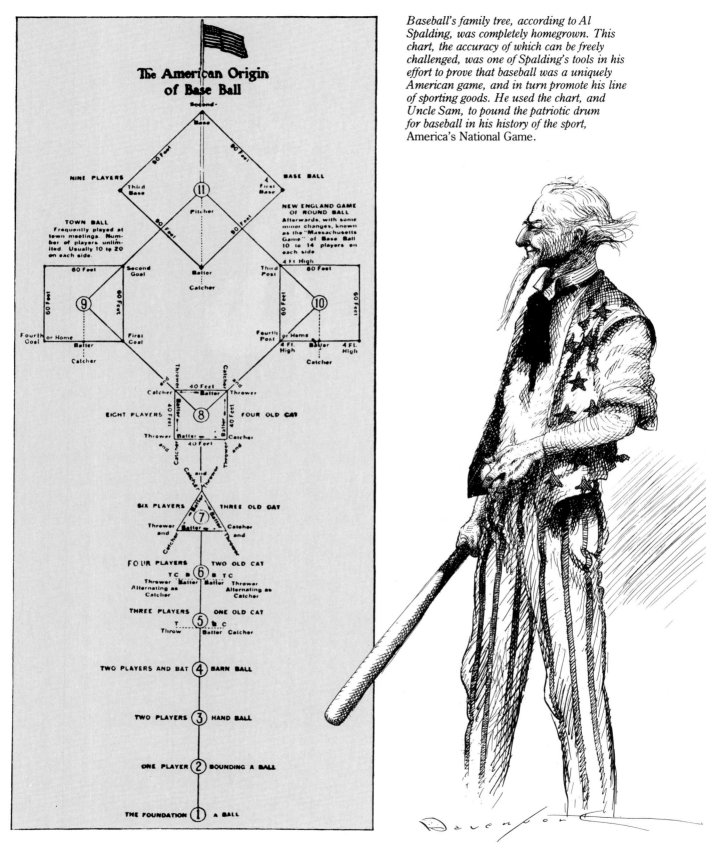

Baseball's family tree, according to Al Spalding, was completely homegrown. This chart, the accuracy of which can be freely challenged, was one of Spalding's tools in his effort to prove that baseball was a uniquely American game, and in turn promote his line of sporting goods. He used the chart, and Uncle Sam, to pound the patriotic drum for baseball in his history of the sport, America's National Game.

returned. If someone caught the hit on the fly, that fielder came in to hit. The batter could also be put out by being "plunked," as Graves put it. If he made it safely, he stayed at bat. The "tosser" stood close to the batter and tossed the ball "straight upward about six feet for the batsman to strike at on its fall"—making the game sound like a cross between slow-pitch softball and hitting fungoes.

Graves said that Doubleday "improved" this primitive game in several ways. First, he made it a team sport with definite sides. Second, he limited the number of players on a side to 11—not 9—to avoid collisions and injuries. Third, he established that there would be four bases, not just two goals.

But the improved game that Graves recalled still allowed "plunking," and was much closer to town ball than to the true baseball developed in New York City a few years later. Even if one of the Doubleday cousins did restructure the game played by the Cooperstown boys, he hadn't invented anything close to modern baseball.

The Knickerbockers were never entirely forgotten, and today they're generally credited as the originators of the modern game. But even in the face of "incontrovertible facts," as Father Chadwick would have put it, the Doubleday myth lives on. Why? Partly because myth is more potent than fact, partly because of the very name itself. Al Spalding happened to choose not just a general who would appeal to our patriotism, but one whose old-fashioned name—Abner Doubleday—resonated with the uncomplicated virtues of a rural America that was fast disappearing: sturdiness, steadiness, independence, honesty. If baseball had needed a symbolic creator, no advertising agency or public relations firm could have done more to create the right image for the game. ⬤

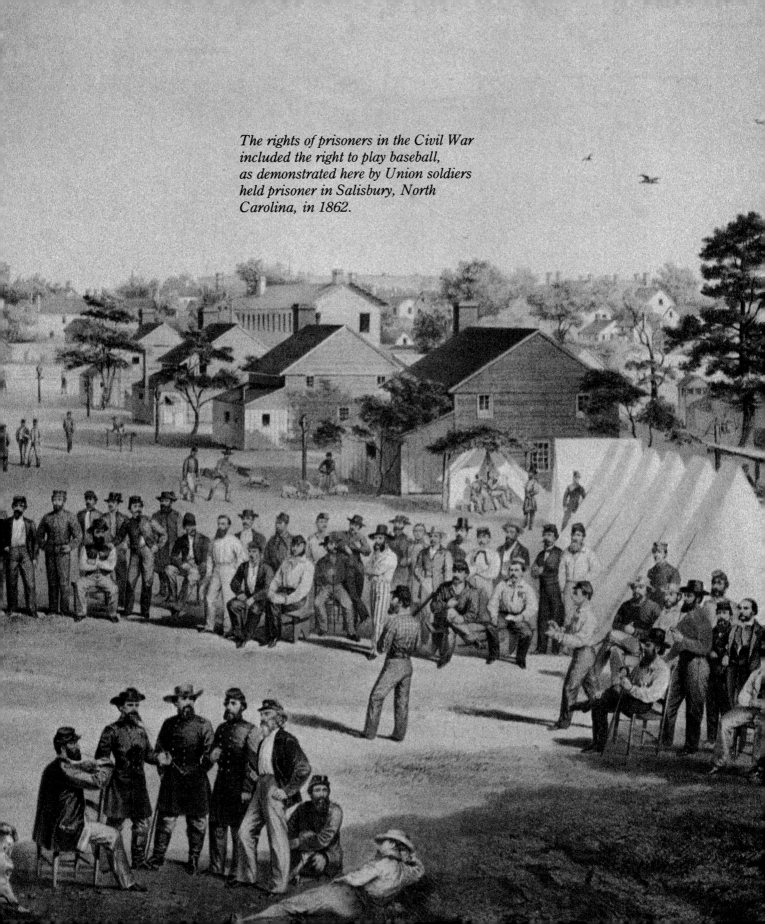

The rights of prisoners in the Civil War included the right to play baseball, as demonstrated here by Union soldiers held prisoner in Salisbury, North Carolina, in 1862.

Al Spalding

The Spalding legacy began, fittingly, with a rolling ball, one that got away from some young players on a field and ended up at the feet of a tall, gangly 12-year-old with oversized ears. Albert Spalding, as expected, tossed the ball back to the infield and, in so doing, launched his career. The throw was so hard and so true that the players immediately invited the youngster to join their team. With that, Al Spalding found baseball. Or more important, baseball found him.

Few men did more to jolt the game from a small-town diversion to the national pastime—first as a player, then as a league official and promoter. In the early days of the sport, Spalding's ideas and dynamism kept it moving ahead and growing with the country. Later his sporting goods company grew with the game and first showed how baseball could beget big business.

The Civil War was winding down when young Spalding made his debut with a teenagers' club team in Rockford, Illinois. Almost immediately he became the team's star pitcher and soon thereafter outgrew the competition. In a challenge game, the Rockford teenagers beat one of the town's adult teams, thanks largely to Spalding's holding the older opponents to only two runs—this at a time when games typically went to 20 or more runs a side. Watching the game were several players from Rockford's top adult team, the Forest Citys, and they wasted no time in inviting the 15-year-old pitcher to join their club. Fortunately, the principal of his school was a baseball fan and gave Spalding permission to leave early every day so he could make his games.

Spalding promptly became the best pitcher the town had seen, and on July 25, 1867, at 16, he pitched a game that made him a sensation. His opponents were the Washington Nationals, the top team in the country, and they were in the midst of a tour of what were then considered western cities. The Nationals had made quick work of teams in Cincinnati, Louisville, Indianapolis and St. Louis and had scheduled the Forest Citys as a warm-up for a game against the Chicago Excelsiors, the team expected to provide the eastern club with its stiffest competition. After a rough start, Spalding held the powerhouse Nationals in check and the Forest Citys scored a stunning 29–23 upset. Spalding's accomplishment became that much more impressive the next day when the Nationals regained their form to demolish the Excelsiors, 49–4. East Coast papers raved about the farmboy who had conquered the big-city bruisers. And the Excelsiors, stinging from their embarrassing defeat, made Spalding an offer he couldn't refuse. They set him up in a job with a Chicago grocer at the then-hefty salary of $40 a week, ten times what he had made in Rockford. It was a sham, of course; his real job was to pitch for the Excelsiors, but players were still supposed to pretend that they played only for the sport of it.

But the grocer went broke—probably from the number of baseball players on the payroll—and Spalding returned to Rockford and the Forest Citys. His reputation kept growing, however, and in 1871 he was lured to Boston with the offer of a $1,500 salary. If Spalding wasn't a national baseball hero already, his stint with the Boston Red Stockings made him one. The fans loved to watch his odd motion

Al Spalding was born to pitch, and he realized it from his very first outing. Spalding modestly claimed that he pitched "as swiftly and nearly as accurately in my first effort as I was ever able to do afterward." In 1872 he led Boston to its first National Association pennant with a 37–8 record and a career-high .339 batting average.

—before each pitch he held the ball with both hands under his chin and spread his feet like a ballet dancer—and his dramatic and effective change-up, which kept batters wildly off-balance. He pitched almost every day in his first year with Boston, appearing in 31 games and winning 20 of them. Then he got comfortable, winning 37 in 1872, 41 in 1873 and 52 in 1874. In 1875 he switched to first base and to the outfield for several games, yet he still won 57 of the 66 games he pitched.

For all his talent, Spalding had even more ambition. He saw great things in baseball's future and he was not shy about staking his claim. Negotiating for the 1876 season, the president of the White Stockings, William Hulbert, offered Spalding a salary increase to come back to Chicago. Once again Spalding went for the better deal, only this time he wasn't just a player switching teams; he was in on the creation of the National League. Hulbert started the new league, and Spalding had access to Hulbert.

Now a league organizer and the Chicago team's manager, Spalding was still baseball's pitching ace. He hurled shutouts in his first two games with his new team and finished the season with 47 wins, a 1.75 ERA and a .312 batting average. By the following season, however, his arm was feeling the effects of too many innings—not to mention that he couldn't master baseball's latest invention, the curveball. In 1878 the first pitcher in history to win 200 games played just one game—as an infielder. His playing days were over, but in some ways, his life was just beginning.

Still in his twenties, he formed the A.G. Spalding & Bros. Company, a sporting goods firm designed to cash in on baseball's newfound popularity. Spalding agreed to provide free baseballs to the National League and, in fact, paid the league a dollar for every dozen balls it used. Not surprisingly, he shut out the competition, and Spalding was able to market his "official ball" to amateur teams all over America. The company strengthened its ties to the league even more when it paid a premium to publish the official NL record book.

While still with Boston, Spalding had helped Harry Wright arrange a much-publicized exhibition schedule in Britain. The British did not seem much impressed, but Spalding was not discouraged. Now that the worldwide spread of baseball was in his best business interests, he took the game to Australia and

At the tender age of 16, Spalding (third from right) was the star pitcher for the Forest City, Illinois, club in 1867. After he got the win in a 29–23 triumph over the vaunted Washington Nationals, a local paper called Spalding "undoubtedly the best pitcher in the West."

organized an exhibition tour in Europe. He had become the game's biggest booster and its biggest entrepreneur. He influenced it in other ways, too, designing an agreement between the NL and teams in small towns that eventually led to the creation of the minor leagues. He led the fight against an attempt to syndicate the league, which would have allowed a handful of people to own all of the teams. And in 1890 he almost singlehandedly won a battle of wills with the players' union after the union called a players' strike.

In time, Spalding was recognized as baseball's elder statesman, publishing its first serious—if somewhat prejudiced—history, *America's National Game,* in 1911. He even ran for one of California's seats in the U.S. Senate as "the Baseball Candidate" in 1910, losing a close race. He died in 1915 and, to no one's surprise, was voted into the Hall of Fame in 1939. After all, his name was on the ball.

More than anyone else, Spalding nurtured the development of professional baseball in its critical first few decades. Upon his death in 1915, the National League issued formal resolutions calling him "the Father and Savior of Baseball" and the game's "first and greatest missionary and propagandist."

AL
SPALDING

Right-Handed Pitcher
Rockford Forest Citys 1866–1871
National Association
Boston Red Stockings 1871–1875
National League
Chicago White Stockings 1876–1878
Hall of Fame 1939

GAMES	**411**
WINS	
Career	255
Season High	57
LOSSES	
Career	69
Season High	18
WINNING PERCENTAGE	
Career	.787
Season High	.919
INNINGS (NL only)	539⅔
ERA (NL only)	
Career	1.78
Season Low	1.75
GAMES STARTED (NL only)	
Career	61
Season High	60
COMPLETE GAMES (NL only)	
Career	53
Season High	53
SHUTOUTS (NL only)	
Career	8
Season High	8
STRIKEOUTS (NL only)	
Career	41
Season High	39
WALKS (NL only)	
Career	26
Season High	26

Combined NA and NL stats unless otherwise noted

The New York Game

This lithograph of New York City in 1866 contains one of the earliest representations of a baseball game. At bottom left is the Elysian Fields in Hoboken, New Jersey, home field of the Knickerbocker nine, authors of baseball's first formal set of rules.

Baseball's first team photo was actually an 1846 metal-backed daguerreotype and featured Alexander Cartwright (back row, center) and his Knickerbocker teammates. The driving force behind the Knickerbockers, Cartwright (below) went west in search of gold in 1849 and introduced baseball to San Francisco and later to Hawaii.

magine a good-sized grassy field surrounded by a growing city. Commercial buildings are going up nearby, and a railway cut forms one boundary. Young men in street clothes—jackets and waistcoats tossed aside, shirtsleeves rolled up—laugh and chatter as they toss a ball around and hit flies to each other, getting ready for a game. These aren't the Knickerbockers—not yet. And the game they're loosening up for at the foot of New York City's Murray Hill isn't quite baseball. But it will be soon. It's summer, 1845.

These fellows are middle-class businessmen by and large—Wall Streeters, some of them. They have been turning out to play ball for at least three years, at first on a corner lot downtown at Madison Avenue and 27th Street. They make great claims for the health benefits of outdoor exercise, but they clearly love the play itself, not to mention their after-game socializing.

The game these young men were playing was town ball of one type or another, but during the season of 1845, something happened. Exactly what happened, we'll never know, but what we're sure of is this: by September 1845 a number of the regular Murray Hill ballplayers had formed a club, calling it the Knickerbocker Base Ball Club, probably after a volunteer fire company some of them had belonged to. The Knickerbockers then published the first written rules of a game distinct from the town ball games of the era—a game that seems a bit primitive to modern eyes, perhaps, but is nonetheless recognizable as real baseball.

The man credited with establishing the Knickerbockers was a dark, handsome 25-year-old named Alexander Joy Cartwright. Standing over six feet tall and weighing more than 200 pounds, the bearded Cartwright was a

Along with settling disputes, umpires in 1847 handed out fines for swearing, as this page from a Knickerbocker scorebook shows. According to historians Joel Zoss and John Bowman, however, "such fines were levied in good spirits by umpires who were in fact friends and fellow players."

giant for his time, and he was by all accounts a skilled and popular ballplayer. Nineteenth-century journalist and sports historian Charles A. Peverelly wrote that Cartwright "one day upon the field proposed a regular organization" of ballplayers, "promising to obtain several recruits."

Because Cartwright urged the formation of the Knickerbockers, and because his grandson wrote to the Baseball Hall of Fame nearly a hundred years later asserting that his grandfather had drawn up the first set of rules, Cartwright is generally considered to be the man who did what Abner Doubleday was given credit for: "inventing" baseball. He even has a plaque at Cooperstown to show for it:

ALEXANDER JOY CARTWRIGHT, JR.
"FATHER OF MODERN BASEBALL"
SET BASES 90 FEET APART.
ESTABLISHED 9 INNINGS AS GAME
AND 9 PLAYERS AS TEAM. ORGANIZED
THE KNICKERBOCKER BASEBALL CLUB
OF N.Y. IN 1845. CARRIED BASEBALL
TO PACIFIC COAST AND HAWAII
IN PIONEER DAYS.

Cartwright was a true pioneer of the game, and his Cooperstown plaque comes much closer to the truth than does the myth of Abner Doubleday, but there's no real evidence that he showed up at the club one day waving a sheet of new rules. In fact, Duncan F. Curry, first president of the Knickerbockers, recalled that it was a Mr. Wadsworth—and not Cartwright—who

The New York Knickerbockers (left of the umpire in the top hat) and the Brooklyn Excelsiors (right of the umpire) were two of baseball's first clubs. By the time this photo was taken, in 1858, baseball could count about 25 clubs, and one of the game's most influential figures, Harry Wright (sixth from left), had begun his playing career.

one day arrived with a diagram of a new field. "The plan caused a great deal of talk," according to Curry, "but finally we agreed to try it."

And there's one more thing: the Knickerbockers weren't really the first baseball club. A note in the *New York Herald* during the fall of 1845 mentioned that the New York Club celebrated its second anniversary on November 11 of that year—placing its founding two years before the Knickerbockers'. In later years, Cartwright himself confirmed the existence of the New York Club in a letter he wrote to an old clubmate. But he argued that the Knickerbockers were still "the first Base Ball Club of N.Y., truly the first, for the old New York Club never had a regular organization." Still, the New York Club was organized enough to hold at least two matches with a Brooklyn team in 1845—almost a year before they played the Knickerbockers in what has been considered the first baseball game between organized clubs.

Who were these New York Club men? They were probably another bunch of young fellows who played regularly at Murray Hill—friends of the future Knickerbockers, who had a hand in developing the rules that made baseball distinct from rounders and town ball.

The changes that allowed baseball to emerge from those old-fashioned children's games were probably not the result of farsightedness. They were almost certainly the result of the Murray Hill players reacting to their own circumstances. Foul territory—which was largely absent from both town ball and cricket—was probably established because the Murray Hill playing site was being squeezed by a glue factory on one side and a railway on the other. And the casual nature of the game meant that the bases were marked on the ground—by caps, bags or flat stones just as they are on

sandlots today—rather than by the posts of rounders and town ball that had to be carried to and from the field. It's ironic to think that baseball, with its bucolic associations, may have been shaped by the booming growth of our largest city.

It's almost certain that the rules were developed, or at least experimented with, before the Knickerbockers came into being, and it's likely that the club had to pick and choose among various ideas and suggestions. Given Cartwright's standing among his friends and the force of character he displayed later in life, he was probably a leader in that effort. But *the* father of modern baseball? Probably not.

What were these so-called Knickerbocker Rules, and how did they create modern baseball out of the town ball, round ball and goal ball being played all over the country? First, and this may be the mysterious Mr. Wadsworth's contribution, the bases were set out in a diamond. This was actually a reversion, not a revolution. Most varieties of town ball were played in a square, with the batter standing halfway between the first and fourth bases, the runners running counterclockwise. The basic layout in rounders was a diamond, and the players ran clockwise.

On the new baseball diamond, the distance from home to second was 42 paces. At three feet per pace, that works out to 126 feet, remarkably close to the current 127 feet, 3⅜ inches. So right from the beginning, the New York game was close to the current 90 feet between bases instead of the 60 feet or so that was more common in other bat-and-ball games at the time. Alexander Cartwright's grandson claimed that his grandfather was responsible for this innovation.

With a proper sense of history, some clubs celebrated their founding by making tokens commemorating the event. These two marked the birth of the Pioneer Base Ball Club of Springfield, Massachusetts, in 1858.

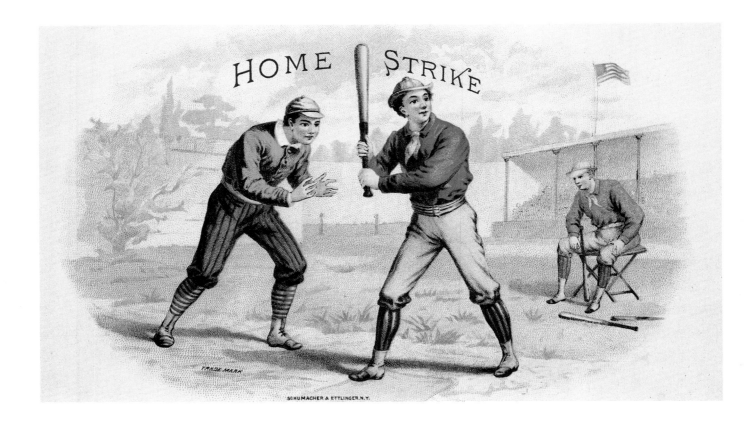

HOME STRIKE

The game's terminology evolved along with the game itself in the 19th century, and at times both were confusing. This tobacco label refers to a "Home Strike," which may have been another term for a home run.

Next, the Knickerbockers established that balls hit outside the first- and third-base lines were foul balls. As they put it, no "ace or base" on a foul ball. By creating an area where play would *not* take place, the Knickerbockers unintentionally created a space from which the game could be conveniently watched. This played a large part in the game's future as a spectator sport.

Under the Knickerbocker rules, the ball had to be pitched underhand with a straight elbow and wrist. A runner could advance on a balk. A batter was out on three strikes, unless the catcher did not handle the ball cleanly. If the catcher dropped the ball, the batter could run to first. The dropped third strike rule is still a part of baseball, as Mickey Owen could attest to his sorrow.

The Knickerbockers decreed that a batting order must be set and stuck to, and they established three outs to an inning. This was the case in some versions of town ball, too, but in others, a single out put the whole team out, or—as in cricket—the entire side had to be retired before the inning was over. For a while, games were played until one team scored 21 "aces," or runs, rather than over a specific number of innings.

But the really key rule change—probably the most important advance made by the lads on Murray Hill—was the one that did away with retiring the runner by hitting him with a thrown ball. Instead of plugging or soaking the runner, the Knickerbockers instituted tagging the runner or the base with the ball to put him out.

Although this change was probably just an intelligent reaction to the prospect of getting a ball in the face, it was vital to the future of the game. With no soaking, a harder ball could be used. A harder ball could be hit farther and more sharply, which in turn required better fielding skills and strategies.

A chromolithograph from the 1864 American Boys Book of Sports and Games *provides one of the earliest scenes of baseball in color. This game featured rocks for bases, a large flag behind home plate and a crowd of well-dressed fans.*

Tagging a runner or a base for an out also led to more sophisticated tactics, precise positioning, and team play that helped make baseball the subtle, complicated, maddening and satisfying game it has become.

The "tag-out" rule altered both the appearance and the feeling of the game. Thirty years later, an English newspaper writer commented about how childlike it is to throw balls at people and how much more manly a game the Americans had made of old rounders. Clearly, modern baseball began as a young man's game—one that was clearly different from the children's ball-games that relied on nailing the runner.

In September 1845, 28 Knickerbockers took the Barclay Street ferry across the Hudson River to play their first informal game at the Elysian Fields in Hoboken, New Jersey. The Elysian Fields was a commercial venture, something like a modern picnic grove, owned by Colonel John Stevens. Since Stevens also owned the ferry service, he looked kindly on ways to woo more New Yorkers over to New Jersey's healthful environs. The Knickerbockers secured the use of the Elysian Fields, including a dressing room, for an annual fee of $75. Evidence suggests that the New York Club had preceded the Knickerbockers to New Jersey, and that the new club may simply have been following the advice of their friends that the Elysian Fields was a fine place to play ball.

Despite the name, all wasn't charm and sylvan beauty at the Elysian Fields. The area was surrounded by taverns, which, according to Mrs. Trollope, an English visitor, "blast the sense for a moment by reeking forth the fumes of whiskey and tobacco." The spot had a reputation as something of a trysting place, as well. George Templeton Strong, a proper New York dia-

Town ball players from Camden, New Jersey, ridiculed for engaging in what some saw as a childish pursuit, joined a group from Philadelphia in 1833 to form the Olympic Town Ball Club (above), recognized by many historians as America's first ballclub.

rist, complained that "its groves are sacred to Venus and I saw scarce any one there but snobs and their strumpets." He also claimed he had to watch his step lest he trip over couples engaged in "the commission of gross vulgarity."

Two years before the Knickerbockers headed for Hoboken, the grossest vulgarian of them all, P. T. Barnum, put on a mock buffalo hunt that got out of hand when the buffalo got loose and scattered the crowd of 30,000. But the Elysian Fields was best known for baseball, and by 1859 eight New York area clubs were playing there regularly. The Knickerbockers shared the area with the Mutuals and Washingtons on Mondays and Thursdays. The Gothams and Eagles played there on Tuesdays and Fridays. And the Empires, the St. Nicholas Club and the Hobokens took their exercise on Wednesdays and Saturdays.

Hoboken and the Elysian Fields were eventually overwhelmed by industrial progress and population growth, but there were still ballfields on the site as late as the 1910s, and big league teams often came to Hoboken for exhibition games in the early part of this century.

Over the years the Knickerbockers have been given credit as the first baseball club, not just because the New York Club wasn't well organized, but because the Knickerbockers kept a series of scorebooks of their matches. These scorebooks still exist. The first one begins in October 1845 and ends on November 18. Whatever else the Knickerbockers were, they must have been a hardy crew.

Early 20th-century writers often characterized the original Knickerbockers as pompous, stiff-necked elitists who didn't want to mix with the rabble. This is nonsense. The Knickerbockers were, at the beginning, a

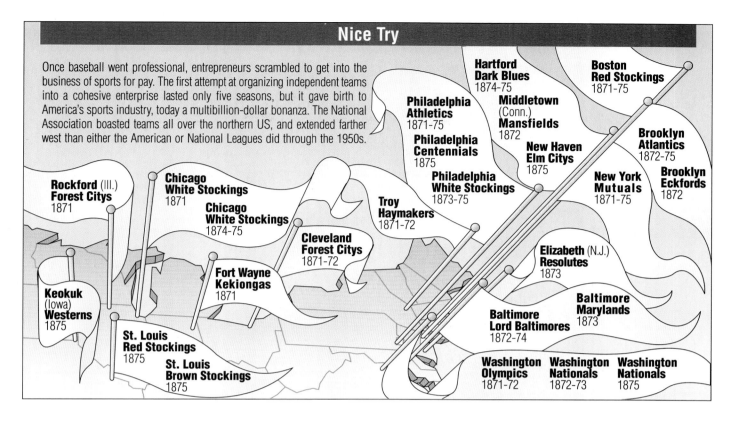

Nice Try

Once baseball went professional, entrepreneurs scrambled to get into the business of sports for pay. The first attempt at organizing independent teams into a cohesive enterprise lasted only five seasons, but it gave birth to America's sports industry, today a multibillion-dollar bonanza. The National Association boasted teams all over the northern US, and extended farther west than either the American or National Leagues did through the 1950s.

Hartford Dark Blues 1874-75

Boston Red Stockings 1871-75

Philadelphia Athletics 1871-75

Middletown (Conn.) Mansfields 1872

Brooklyn Atlantics 1872-75

Philadelphia Centennials 1875

New Haven Elm Citys 1875

New York Mutuals 1871-75

Brooklyn Eckfords 1872

Rockford (Ill.) Forest Citys 1871

Chicago White Stockings 1871

Philadelphia White Stockings 1873-75

Chicago White Stockings 1874-75

Troy Haymakers 1871-72

Cleveland Forest Citys 1871-72

Keokuk (Iowa) Westerns 1875

Fort Wayne Kekiongas 1871

Elizabeth (N.J.) Resolutes 1873

Baltimore Maryland 1873

St. Louis Red Stockings 1875

Baltimore Lord Baltimores 1872-74

St. Louis Brown Stockings 1875

Washington Olympics 1871-72

Washington Nationals 1872-73

Washington Nationals 1875

---

group of hearty, fun-loving young men who thrived in the bustling, growing city of New York. They were men of commerce and the professions, yet in 1849 Alexander Cartwright himself, one of their founders and guiding lights, took off for the West when news about the gold strike in California hit town.

Nonetheless, it's always been something of a joke that the Knickerbockers, the so-called originators of the sport, lost the so-called first baseball game between clubs to the New York Club by a score of 23–1. The implication was that the Knickerbockers were such dilettantes that they couldn't even play their own game well enough to keep from being slaughtered by a pickup team of town ball players and cricketers. But this, too, is misleading. The Knickerbockers didn't play their best team against the New York Club; Cartwright, for example, wasn't in the lineup. And it's clear now that members of the New York Club—who, even though they weren't as organized, had two years more experience than their rivals—were just as involved in the development of the game as the Knickerbockers. This legendary first game was essentially a social event among friends who had been playing ball together for years, and who went on doing so afterward. When the New York Club disintegrated by the end of 1846, several of its members joined the Knickerbockers. And only a few days after the famous first game, the Knickerbockers played one of their typical intraclub games, with several New York Club players in the lineup on each side.

This arrangement was actually quite common for the KBC, as its members called the club. The Knickerbockers—amateurs all—played virtually all their games among themselves, a pattern that held true for all clubs that began during the 1850s. Matches with other clubs were the exception, not the rule.

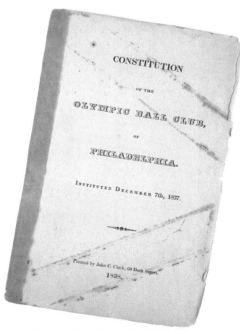

For 27 years the Olympic Ball Club of Philadelphia played town ball, then adopted the National Association of Base Ball Players' game of baseball in 1860. The switch increased the distance between the bases from 60 to 90 feet and caused the retirement of many of the team's older players.

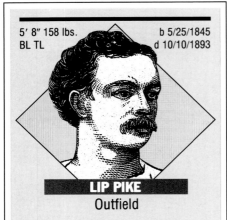

5' 8" 158 lbs.
BL TL

b 5/25/1845
d 10/10/1893

LIP PIKE
Outfield

Lipman Pike was a speedy, sure-handed fielder, a heavy hitter, and probably the first Jewish professional baseball player and manager. Known as "the Iron Batter," Pike compiled a .321 average in 260 National Association games and a .304 average in 163 National League games. He moved frequently and never played for the same team for more than two years in his 17-year career.

Although he was best known as an outfielder, Pike was playing second base for the Brooklyn Atlantics on June 14, 1870, when they put a halt to the Cincinnati Red Stockings' 92-game winning streak. Pike occasionally took on the role of player-manager during his career, but washed his hands of that job for the last time during the 1877 season, when Cincinnati went 3–11 under his leadership.

According to one story, Pike once hit six homers in a single game in Springfield, Massachusetts. The feat seems a bit unlikely, especially since his highest home run total for a whole year was four—enough to lead the NL in 1877. But home runs, and home run hitters, were rare in the 1870s, and Pike had another, more important asset: tremendous speed. In 1873, while he was with the Lord Baltimores, Pike accepted a $250 wager to race a horse —a fast trotter—in a 100-yard dash. The race was held at the team's Newington Park field and was witnessed by a crowd of about 400. Pike ran the distance in ten seconds—and beat the horse by four yards.

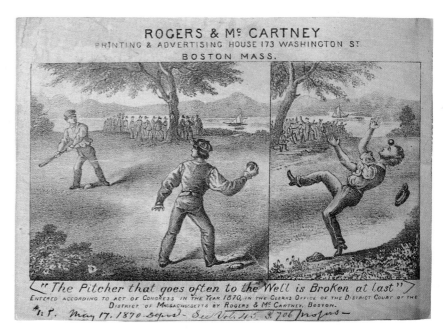

In baseball's early years, the pitcher had more to fear from getting beaned than did the batter, as demonstrated in this 1860s engraving. It wasn't until 1872 that pitchers were allowed to snap their wrists during their delivery.

The Knickerbocker scorebooks show that the club played ball quite often: several times a week on average. Members often got in more than one game a day. They'd choose up teams—"blacks" and "whites"—play to a score of 21 or sometimes 11, then start all over again if they had time. They frequently played with fewer than nine men on a side if there were not enough club members on hand for a match. Far from being exclusive snobs, the Knickerbockers commonly included guests in their intraclub lineups. In fact, in their fancy new 1856 scorebook they included a column headed "Members from other Clubs," a list containing Gothams, Eckfords, Empires, Eagles, Putnams, along with some designated as "none" or "no club." One guest was identified simply as "Cricketer." In 1847 they had a woman umpire, the otherwise anonymous Mrs. Doolittle, surely one of the first female arbiters in the history of the game, but not the last.

The Knickerbockers probably didn't care much that the New York Club beat them so badly. And the New Yorks probably wouldn't have minded if the score had been reversed. To these fellows, baseball was for fun and exercise. They weren't that interested in interclub competition. The Knickerbockers, in fact, didn't play another match game until 1851.

By then a number of clubs had been formed, and throughout the decade club baseball boomed in New York. Inevitably, the new clubs began to compete for dominance. The Knickerbockers actually discussed recruiting outstanding players, but a majority of the membership remained committed to the original ideas of exercise and good fellowship. Nonetheless, the club remained an important force in New York baseball through the 1850s.

For a while, the Knickerbockers remained in the forefront of the devel-

opment of the rules, too. According to their original rules, fielders could put a batter out by catching a batted ball on the first bounce. The Knickerbockers realized by the mid-1850s that the game would be stronger and require sharper skills if a fly ball had to be caught in the air for an out. They agitated for years before the rule was finally changed in 1858. And they gave frequent demonstrations of the superiority of the "fly rule," announcing in 1859 that *their* games would be played using the new, more demanding rule.

The Knickerbockers stayed together long enough to build a new clubhouse at the Elysian Fields in the early 1870s, but they finally expired a decade later. By then, the professional game was thoroughly established, and even amateur nines played for keeps. The Knickerbockers—who remained true to the creed of playing for fun—were already looking anachronistic and more than a little silly. But they'd been present at the creation, they'd put the rules on paper and they'd fought to improve the sport. No question about it. Their game is our game. ⊕

There are several contenders for the title "baseball's first game," but one of the leaders is the game between the Knickerbockers and a team known as the New York Club at the Elysian Fields on June 19, 1846 (above). Some reports indicate Alexander Cartwright wasn't there; others claim he was the game's umpire. In any case, his Knickerbockers got pounded, 23–1.

Jim Creighton

Baseball has had its share of heroes, men who defined the game, reshaped it, somehow made it bigger than sport. In their own ways, they made the most of their time on the field, from Ty Cobb to Babe Ruth to Joe DiMaggio, from Jackie Robinson to Hank Aaron to Reggie Jackson.

But before them all came James Creighton, America's first—and probably purest—baseball hero. Born in New York in 1841, he was already recognized as a star of the game by his 19th birthday. The son of a city hall clerk, Creighton started playing with local ballclubs, which were formed by players, mostly merchants and businessmen, for exercise in the spirit of good, clean sportsmanship. But Creighton's unique talents brought a sharper competitive edge to the game.

Creighton, a lanky teenager, began his career in 1858 as an infielder with the Niagara Club of Brooklyn; the borough was then the hotbed of baseball. He shot into stardom, however, when he moved to the pitcher's box the next year. At the time pitchers were required to deliver the ball underhanded with a stiff arm, but Creighton wasn't satisfied with the result and proceeded to raise the art of pitching several notches. Instead of flipping the ball softly, he fired it toward the plate, his pitching hand dipping down near the ground and rising upward sharply. On top of that, he snapped his wrist, causing the ball to spin—and creating the precursor of the curveball. From 45 feet away—then the distance from the front of the pitcher's box to home—the effect was devastating. His "speed ball" pitches, according to one writer of the time, were as "swift as they could be sent from a cannon." Soon he began mixing the pace of his pitches, keeping the already overwhelmed batters off-balance. The result was that most of them either struck out or popped up.

Purists were outraged; Creighton, they charged, was violating the spirit of the game. But their protests were in vain. Once other clubs saw how overpowering Creighton could be, they wanted him—and his technique—for themselves. In fact, the first team Creighton pitched against, the Brooklyn Stars, immediately snatched him away. Within a year, he was grabbed by the powerful Excelsior Club of Brooklyn.

Creighton's switch to part-time pitcher had no effect on the other parts of his game. He remained a remarkable hitter and a good fielder. Pitchers rarely spent all their playing time in the pitcher's box, and Creighton also played the infield and, occasionally, the outfield. The New York papers gave him credit for starting what may have been the sport's first triple play. According to published reports, Creighton was in left field for the July 22, 1860, game between the Brooklyn Excelsiors and the Baltimore Excelsiors. With none out and men on second and third, he made a one-handed catch of a long fly ball, followed by a perfect throw to third to catch the runner off base. The third baseman quickly threw to second, and the second baseman tagged the runner to complete the triple play.

But it was Creighton's pitching that made the Brooklyn Excelsiors practically unbeatable in 1860 and 1861. The club is generally acknowledged to have made Creighton the first paid baseball player, but since the National Association of Base Ball Players forbade payments to players, the arrangements were not made public. The club may have given him money, or they may have found him a job.

JAMES CREIGHTON,

Pitcher of the EXCELSIOR BASE BALL CLUB of Brooklyn, N. Y.

Although Jim Creighton was best known as a pitcher, perhaps his most remarkable feat came at the plate; he is credited by several historians as being the only player ever to play an entire season without making a single out.

The first pitcher to overpower hitters with his speed, Creighton unfortunately was also the first player to die from hitting a ball too hard. The resulting injury killed him at age 21. His tombstone in Brooklyn, wrote Al Spalding, "would never be mistaken for anything else than the grave of a ball player."

With the pitching star on their team, the Excelsiors became the first to go on an extensive tour, traveling to upstate New York, Pennsylvania, Delaware, Maryland and even Canada, drawing big crowds and destroying almost every local team that dared to face them. A team in Buffalo fell by a score of 50–19; another, in Baltimore, surrendered 51–6. Even a team of New York all-star players didn't stand a chance, despite the fact that they were permitted 18 men in the field and six outs an inning—the Excelsiors manhandled them, 45–16. The team was becoming an East Coast legend, and none of its players more so than Creighton. James D'Wolff Lovett, captain of a Boston club, said, "Creighton had a great influence upon my success as a pitcher. I noted him very carefully and found that his speed was not due to mere physical strength, but that this later was supplemented by a very long arm and a peculiar wrist movement, very quick and snappy." Pitchers with many clubs began mimicking his wicked motion; some teams even named themselves after him.

When Creighton (third from left) joined the Excelsiors in 1860, the team went from good to great, on the field and at the box office. With other stars like Asa Brainard (second from right), the Excelsiors drew crowds of more than 10,000 for each game of a three-game series against the Atlantics.

JIM CREIGHTON

Outfielder, Right-Handed Pitcher
Brooklyn Niagaras 1858–1859
Brooklyn Stars 1859
Brooklyn Excelsiors 1860–1862

Not all baseballs were created equal in the game's early days, but no matter whether the ball had a lead or rubber core, Jim Creighton could throw it faster than just about anyone else.

At the peak of Creighton's stardom, in October 1862, he came to bat against the Unions of Morrisania, a New York City club. He lunged at a pitch; a loud pop sounded just before his bat hit the ball. The result was a home run, and Creighton rounded the bases. When he crossed the plate he told a teammate, "I must have snapped my belt." What he had done was rupture his bladder. He passed out on the field and was carried to his father's house in Brooklyn. After several days of internal hemorrhaging, Creighton died, six months shy of his 22nd birthday.

His teammates, stricken with grief, paid homage to him in the only way they thought fitting. Above his grave in Brooklyn's Greenwood Cemetery they erected a tall granite monument bedecked with the symbols of his sport: two crossed bats, a base, a cap, even a scorebook. At the very top of the column rests a stone baseball. Everyone, they felt, should know that this was the final resting place of a man who was not just a baseball player, but the game's first superstar.

For Health and Recreation

"Well—it's our game; America's game; has the snap, go, fling of the American atmosphere; it belongs as much to our institutions, fits into them as significantly, as our constitution's laws; is just as important as the sum total of our historic life."
—Walt Whitman on baseball

By the 1850s, baseball was flourishing—at least in New York. Enthusiasts rushing to take up the new sport made a run on equipment, and as a result, bats and balls were in short supply. A June 1857 notice in the *New York Clipper* announced that "of late we have had considerable enquiry for balls, bats & c., used in the game of Base Ball, but as those who have them for sale keep quiet on the subject, we have been unable to give the information." An even better barometer of the game's success were the large numbers of spectators who regularly turned out to watch interclub matches. Describing a game between the Gotham and Atlantic Clubs at the Elysian Fields on October 30, 1857, the *Clipper* reported that "the Hoboken ferry boats added largely to their number of passengers, while the road leading to the grounds by the river side was crowded by persons, wending their way to witness the always exciting match. By the time it began, the playing grounds . . . were densely packed by spectators, barely leaving sufficient room for the prosecution of the beautiful game."

The Knickerbockers and other local baseball clubs were all playing more or less the same game, but it was becoming obvious that some adjustments were in order. In May of 1857 representatives of 16 clubs got together in Manhattan to modify and standardize the rules. The most important change was adopting the now-familiar nine-inning rule. It replaced the Knickerbockers' original dictum that the first team to score 21 runs, or "aces," won

By the early 1870s, baseball was quilted into the fabric of American life (opposite). In 1873 Birchard Hayes wrote to his father, President Rutherford B. Hayes, "one reason for my dread of life after leaving College is because I will be unable to play ball."

ADMISSION SEASON TICKET.
PRICE $2.00.

International Cricket Matches

MATCH.
L ENGLAND ELEVEN," Oct. 3, 5, 6.

MATCH.
GLAND ELEVEN," Oct. 8, 9, 10.

(If practicable.)
ENGLAND" NINE, Oct. 12.

day at 11 o'clock.

NINTH AND GREEN STREETS.
may be obtained on Exhibiting this Ticket.

FORFEITED IF TRANSFERRED.

Admit

For $2—a hefty price in the 1860s—fans in Philadelphia could enjoy a cross-cultural sporting experience, as a series of cricket matches pitted U.S. clubs—cricket and baseball—against imports from Great Britain.

the game. Even in an era of puff pitching and wild offense, the 21-run rule had been turning too many games into marathon contests. The nine-inning rule was just one of the hundreds of rule changes that eventually transformed a simple gentlemen's sport into the intricate and intense modern game.

The sport was booming, and as early as 1857, Porter's *Spirit of the Times,* in an early example of Manhattan media bombast, called baseball "a national pastime." But even the New York papers realized that it wasn't yet *the* national pastime. Nevertheless, matches were regularly covered in the press, and colorful descriptions replaced simple box scores, as in this summary of yet another game between the Gothams and the Atlantics: "The Atlantics now tried their hands at the hickory for a second time, and excellent use they made of it, man after man arriving at the home goal and piling on the runs up to number 10. This was tremendous and caused the Gotham gentlemen to think that they had come to the wrong spot to catch weazels asleep."

In 1858 the New York clubs formed the grandly and inaccurately named National Association of Base Ball Players: the first baseball organization in the history of the United States. To the north, New Englanders were still playing a highly evolved version of town ball, often called the Massachusetts game. Probably in reaction to the formation of the National Association in New York, New Englanders held a baseball convention in Dedham, Massachusetts, in 1858. The result was the Massachusetts Association of Base Ball Players. By 1860 this organization counted 32 clubs and had changed its name to the New England Association of Base Ball Players.

But it was too late. A New York-style club had been formed in Boston in 1857, and New England's first Knickerbocker-style baseball game was played on Boston Common the next year. The Massachusetts game simply

wasn't as exciting to play or to watch, and by the start of the Civil War, town ball had lost its battle with the New York game.

Surprisingly, the real contest for dominance wasn't between the New York and Massachusetts games. It was between baseball in any form and cricket. The English sport was actually the country's favorite adult ballgame, at least until the mid-1850s. In 1856, 10,000 spectators crowded the Elysian Fields to watch cricket teams representing New York and Montreal play a match. In the late 1850s, well-known baseball players were joining cricket clubs and competing at the English game, and vice-versa. Historian George Kirsch estimates that by 1860 there were some 400 cricket clubs in the United States, with perhaps 10,000 players. As the Civil War began, it was even money as to whether cricket or the newfangled baseball was the ball-game of choice in the United States.

Wars change men and nations. Knickerbocker baseball emerged from the war as a sport played by all, not just by middle-class New York gents. Baseball was spread by Union soldiers, especially the members of New York regiments. The experience of Nick Young, who later became president of the National League, was probably typical: "In my regiment we had a full cricket team, all of whom had played together at home, and our first match was arranged and played near White Oak Church, Va., in the early spring of 1863, against the Ninety-fifth Pennsylvania Regiment's team, hailing from Philadelphia. About this time a Base Ball club was organized in the Twenty-seventh New York Regiment, so we turned our attention to Base Ball, and kept it up as we had the chance until the close of the war. It was here that I played my first regular game of Base Ball."

In 1859 baseball fans at the Elysian Fields in Hoboken watched games from carriages (bottom), but cricket (top) on the same field drew a bigger crowd. This spread from Harper's Weekly *features one of the earliest drawings of adults playing baseball.*

| 6' 1" 177 lbs. | b July 1845 |
| BR TR | d 11/4/1921 |

LEVI MEYERLE
Infield

"Long Levi" Meyerle was as awe-inspiring with a bat as he was awful with his hands. One of the game's first great sluggers, the Philadelphia hometown favorite was probably the first player evaluated as "good hit, no field." Meyerle tried every position save catcher, but the batter's box was the only place he was at home.

In 1871 Meyerle captured the first National Association batting title with an astounding .492 average and also led the league with four homers. He capped the season on October 30 with three hits as his team, the Philadelphia Athletics, beat Chicago, 4–1, to capture the new league's pennant. During his five years—and 221 games—in the NA, Meyerle hit .353 with 386 hits. In 1876, with the Philadelphia Athletics in the new NL, he pounded out 87 hits in 55 games and had a .340 average. With Cincinnati in 1877, his last full season in the majors, he hit .327.

Unfortunately, Long Levi had to field, too. As a member of the Chicago White Stockings in 1874, he made six errors in a single game. In 1876, playing mostly at third base for Philadelphia of the NL, Meyerle blundered his way to a .790 fielding percentage.

After a severe ankle injury in 1877 further limited his already restricted range in the field, Meyerle began playing in the minor leagues. In 1884 he returned to the majors for three games with Philadelphia's Union Association team. He hit just .091, so he retired from baseball and became a carpenter and painter.

A huge crowd—hardly any of whom paid—watched in delight as their hometown Philadelphia Athletics beat the Brooklyn Atlantics, 31–12, in Game 2 of the 1866 championship series. Brooklyn catcher Charlie Mills had a bad day with 12 passed balls.

Why didn't the baseball players turn to cricket instead of the other way around? There were two very good reasons, neither of which had to do with "national character" or the intrinsic merit of either sport. In the first place, a cricket match could take several days to complete. A baseball game took a couple of hours and appealed to working fellows who had limited free time. This advantage was even recognized by the English. Second, cricket's sophisticated rules and complex techniques were beyond the abilities of boys who hadn't grown up with it. Baseball, while requiring enough skill to interest adult players, could be played casually without a lot of training or knowledge of a rulebook. It was accessible to any man who'd ever played rounders or town ball as a child. The Civil War spread the seeds of the sport west and south, where it blossomed just as it had in the East and Midwest. After Appomattox, the game and the country grew up together.

While soldiers were picking up the sport by the thousands, war put a serious crimp in club baseball in northeastern cities: membership in the National Association fell as low as 28 clubs. But when peace returned in 1865, interest in the game exploded. The next year, more than 200 clubs were represented at the NA's annual convention. Most were clustered in the Northeast, but there were clubs from Tennessee and Virginia in the old Confederacy, and others from Iowa and Oregon. The *New York Herald* declared that "the national game of America is now *par excellence,* baseball."

In August 1867 the National Base Ball Club of Washington, D.C., opened its new grounds in the nation's capital. Thousands showed up that day, and most of them paid a quarter to get in. The guest of honor was Presi-

dent Andrew Johnson, who was shown to a special seat on the balcony of the clubhouse. A few weeks earlier, he had been made an honorary member of the Mutual Club of New York, which was sponsored by the infamous Tammany Hall political machine. Johnson needed respect. The Tennessee Democrat had been under fire from an increasingly hostile Republican Congress and he faced impeachment. In a gathering of supportive "Mutes" at the White House, the President spoke of his fondness for the game, his memories of ballplaying as a young man and of the game's "moral" nature. He also stated presidentially that baseball was the "national game" of the United States. Johnson—the first true fan to live in the White House—was right.

But the game had already changed drastically from what it had been in the 1840s. The Knickerbockers had played ball "for health and recreation merely," as one of their early members put it, and they invariably combined sport with hospitality, laying on picnics and banquets for their friendly opponents. But during the 1850s the attitude changed. Newer clubs began to approach competition for its own sake. Winning became the goal, and bitter rivalries between clubs developed. Teams were even competing to see who could put on the most spectacular feed: "After the conclusion of the match the party adjourned to the Florence House, through the invitation of Mr. Dupignac, there to partake of an excellent banquet, which was much relished, it being the grand finale of a holiday long to be remembered by all." In an attempt to counteract such competition, in 1859 the National Association tried to ban refreshments after games.

As clubs got more serious about winning, money entered the game. Back in 1858, players from Brooklyn clubs met their New York counterparts

Publicity has always been important to baseball, and the New York Clipper *was one of the foremost chronicles of baseball's early years. This woodcut featuring a game between the Gotham and Eagle Clubs at the Elysian Fields was page-one news in its September 19, 1857, edition.*

By 1866 baseball fever was spreading beyond the traditional strongholds of New York and Pennsylvania. At a convention of the National Association of Base Ball Players in New York, 202 clubs from 17 states and the District of Columbia were represented.

5′ 3½″ 161 lbs.
BR TR
b 1/2/1836
d 10/12/1908

DICKEY PEARCE
Shortstop

Dickey Pearce was neither big nor fast; in fact, he was plump and awkward, but he was one of the most inventive players in the 19th century.

Pearce had experience at several positions by 1873, when he joined the Brooklyn Atlantics. The Atlantics made the pudgy player their full-time shortstop, since early shortstops customarily stood on the baseline midway between second and third, moving little. But Pearce became one of the first mobile shortstops; he backed up into the outfield, moved in, and shifted left or right as the situation and his knowledge of the hitters dictated. He also stopped a lot of ground balls—often using his foot—that other infielders let by because they feared injuring their bare fingers.

At the plate, Pearce was equally creative and is generally credited with the invention of both the fair-foul hit and the bunt. His hits were initially ridiculed —other players referred to the bunt as the "baby act." But one reporter of the time wrote, "Take the average of heavy hitters, and you will find that those who go in for the Pearce style possess the best record at the close of the season."

Pearce finished the 1877 season with the St. Louis Browns, then retired from the majors. He played for several minor league teams until an injury ended his playing career, then returned to the majors as an NL umpire.

The 1859 edition of the Atwater Base Ball Club of Westfield, Massachusetts, may not have been the most talented or storied club of the 19th century, but it was without a doubt one of the most fashion-conscious.

in the "Fashion Course Series"—baseball's first all-star contest. Held at a racetrack on Long Island, the games caused a frenzy. Special steamers and extra ferries and stages were laid on to bring crowds from Manhattan, and 4,000 attended the opener of what one paper called "these Yankee Olympian games." Victory went to New York, two games to one. More important, though, those attending were charged 50 cents apiece "to cover the cost of putting the grounds in order." As far as we know, this was the first time anyone ever paid to see a baseball game.

It didn't take sharp minds long to realize that, far from merely covering expenses, real profit could be made from baseball. When the Excelsiors played the Atlantics before 10,000 Brooklynites in 1860, no admission was charged. But in 1862 William Cammeyer made a move that established him as the spiritual patron of baseball entrepreneurs. Cammeyer owned the land that Brooklyn's Union Club played on, and that year he enclosed the field and began charging ten cents admission. He offered the Unions free use of the grounds, which they cheerfully accepted. But the Unions, seeing the money Cammeyer was raking in, demanded—and got—half of his profits the following season.

By the time Andrew Johnson recognized baseball as the national game, most of what were called the "first class" clubs had enclosed their grounds and were charging ten cents or a quarter a head for admission. In 1869 *The New York Times* reported that over 200,000 spectators had seen important matches during the previous seasons, and that the Mutuals alone had earned the fabulous sum of $15,000 in profits.

But it wasn't just the clubs that were making money from the game. By the mid-1860s many players were, too. The arrangement for most of them

River City B.B.C.
1866

Jerry Hall — C.
Sam Harper — 2.nd
Geo Haljenstun — 3.rd
John McMillen — S.S.
Ed Kelley — L.F.
Pat Corbett — 1.st
Bau Sprg — R.E

was what today we would call "semiprofessional": they got a cut of the gate but no regular salary. This led to real problems. As John Montgomery Ward put it in his short history of the game, "the players who were depending on a share of the 'gate' arranged to win or lose a game in order that the deciding contest might draw well." Ward also noted that "baneful influences" had crept into the game: gamblers were winning and losing huge amounts of money on big club matches. "With so much money at stake," wrote Ward, "the public knew that players would be tampered with."

And tampered with they were. The Chicago White Sox of 1919 were not the first team to be reached by gamblers putting in the fix. On September 28, 1865, the favored Mutuals—Tammany's team—lost to the Eckfords. Catcher William Wansley and third baseman Ed Duffy were expelled for throwing the game. Shortstop Thomas Devyr was suspended until 1867. It was baseball's first public scandal and it hurt the game's image badly.

Even under these circumstances, baseball clubs remained just that: clubs, not merely teams. By the mid-1860s, for example, the Athletics of Philadelphia had 419 members. Brooklyn's Excelsiors had 350. And Brooklyn's other great club, the Atlantics, had 220. Obviously, only a few of these members were good enough to play on the club's first team. Others played on the second nine or with the lowly "muffins," who, it can be assumed, muffed many chances in the field. Others never picked up a bat, but supported their club's teams feverishly. It was a lot like—dare we say it?—the system of cricket clubs that exists in Britain to this day.

Yet increasingly competitive baseball dominated the clubs from the late 1850s right through the end of the 1860s. Brooklyn took the lead, with strong

Continued on page 70

If there was trouble in River City in 1866, it probably had something to do with these characters, who made up the River City Base Ball Club in Portsmouth, Ohio.

Union Grounds

Business was brisk in the winter at the Union Skating Club's ice rink in Brooklyn, but rink owner William Cammeyer was looking for some summer income. Brooklyn in 1862 was a baseball hotbed, so Cammeyer, heir to his family's successful leather goods business, built himself a ballpark—America's first enclosed ballpark. Cammeyer located Union Grounds near three streetcar lines, and then he set about creating the ballpark atmosphere and customs that—with some exceptions and alterations—still exist today.

First, he charged admission. On Opening Day in 1862, Cammeyer opened the gates at Union Grounds at no charge to get the locals interested, then later charged ten cents a head. By 1866 demand had allowed Cammeyer to raise the price of admission to 25 cents, and top-flight clubs like the Atlantics drew overflow crowds. Second, he designed a ballpark where fans could watch and players could play free of the chaos that reigned at many other game sites. For the players, Cammeyer built a clubhouse large enough for three teams and maintained the game's finest playing field. Fan rowdiness was not tolerated, allowing the game to proceed "without the slightest interference from outsiders," wrote a reporter for the *Sunday Mercury*. The horseshoe-shaped grandstand was far enough from the diamond that games could be played without the fans interrupting the players, yet the accommodations for those fans were the finest in the land—room for 1,500 on long benches on three sides of the field. Outfield fences were more than 500 feet from home plate. He had

several flagpoles put up to wave team pennants and the American flag, and set aside a place for "The Star Spangled Banner" to be played. Cammeyer sold refreshments—though nothing alcoholic—and separated gamblers, often the source of ballpark mayhem, by giving them their own space, a "bettor's ring" that proved to be one the of ballpark's most popular haunts.

At first, Cammeyer's offer of free rent to three local clubs—the Eckfords, Putnams and Constellations—seemed like a good deal, except that he was pocketing all the admissions. A few years later the Union Nine of Brooklyn demanded a share in the profits, and from then on profit sharing was the rule at Union Grounds. High-profile matchups were also the rule, as the ballpark became the site of most important club matches, even though sometimes neither team hailed from New York City. On June 15, 1869, the unbeaten, unabashedly professional Cincinnati Red Stockings came to Union Grounds to face the Mutuals, New York's finest "amateur" team. The game caused a traffic jam throughout the Williamsburg section of Brooklyn, and the crowd overflowed onto nearby rooftops. Cincinnati won the game, 4–2, then came back a year later, still undefeated, and beat the Mutuals, 16–3.

By 1870 ticket prices for big games had jumped to 50 cents, and in 1871 Union Grounds played host to the National Association championship game between the Philadelphia Athletics and the Chicago White Stockings, which Philadelphia won, 4–1.

Union Grounds hosted several NA and National League teams into the late 1870s, but when the NL's Hartfords—who played their home games there—disbanded at the end of the 1877 season, major league baseball abandoned the ballpark. On May 24, 1889, Brooklyn's entry in the American Association played its only—and the last ever—major league game at Union Grounds.

Manhattan may have housed New York's financial district, but Brooklyn—specifically Union Grounds—was the city's baseball center in the 1860s. The ballpark played host to some of the most important games of the decade.

Union Grounds

Lee Avenue and Rutledge Street
Brooklyn, New York

Built 1862

New York Mutuals, NA
1871–1875
Brooklyn Eckfords, NA
1871–1872
Brooklyn Atlantics, NA
1873–1875

New York Mutuals, NL
1876
Hartfords of Brooklyn, NL
1877

Seating Capacity
1,500

Style
Wooden

Height of Outfield Fences
Between 6 and 7 feet

Distance of Outfield Fences
All over 500 feet

Brooklyn may have been the hub of baseball in 19th-century New York, but the Bronx had some ballplayers too, including the Union Base Ball Club of Morrisania, which in 1866 was among the top teams in the nation. The team featured 19-year-old George Wright (fourth from right) and drew a crowd of 7,000 for an early-season 24–23 loss to the New York Mutuals.

teams representing the Excelsior, Atlantic, Eckford and Union clubs, among others. Across the river in Manhattan, the Mutuals were tough almost every year. Outside the New York area, the strongest team represented the Athletic Club of Philadelphia.

The National Association that these clubs belonged to wasn't a league in the modern sense. It made rules, but it never established schedules. Matches were arranged by the clubs themselves. No club played more than 20 or so games a year, and most played fewer. Nor did the National Association set up any mechanism to decide an annual championship. For a while, the best team was decided by consensus: the Excelsior Club, with pitching ace James Creighton, and the Eckfords, with outfielder Al Reach, were tops in the early 1860s. In 1864 the Atlantics, led by Dickey Pearce—a bare-handed fielding whiz who was the game's first great shortstop—continued Brooklyn's domination of top-flight baseball.

The next year the championship became a little more formal when the Atlantics met the Mutuals at the Elysian Fields in "the first grand match for the championship of the United States." Between 15,000 and 20,000 watched Brooklyn win a game stopped by rain in the sixth, and for the next few years the Atlantics set the standard, becoming the game's earliest legitimate dynasty. They were so good that any best-of-three series with them was considered a championship battle. The Atlantics didn't drop the deciding game of a series until 1867, when the underdog Unions of Morrisania—now part of the Bronx—bushwhacked them in one of the sport's first great upsets.

During their dominance, the Atlantics' strongest rivals were the Athletics, and contests between the two teams attracted huge, highly partisan crowds that demonstrated the popularity of baseball as a spectator

sport. In the fall of 1866, the two teams attracted 8,000 to the Athletics' unenclosed diamond at 15th and Columbia in Philadelphia, collecting 25 cents a head. Outside the grounds, another 30,000 or so climbed trees, stood on chairs, balanced on fences and peered from housetops as the two teams went at it. Gamblers were everywhere, tempers ran high and the crowds got so rowdy that the game had to be called. Two weeks later, the teams met before nearly 20,000 spectators at Brooklyn's Capitoline Grounds. The Atlantics won, 27–17.

Back in Philadelphia the Athletics had put up a fence around their ball field. Three thousand fanatics paid the vast sum of a dollar each to get in, while another 20,000 or so peered and cheered from outside as the hometown Athletics tied the series by winning, 31–12. As was typical in this era, these two great club teams never decided the issue. They fought over the division of gate receipts and never played the final game. The Atlantics remained champs.

The next year the two clubs tried again, with similar results. They split the first two games and were scheduled to meet at Brooklyn's Union Grounds on September 30 for all the marbles. Several Atlantic players had been injured in the previous week's game, though, and the club wired Philadelphia to ask for a postponement. The Athletics either didn't receive the telegram or didn't care to honor it, because they showed up on the 30th ready to play. The Atlantics took a look at the paying crowd that had gathered, and agreed to a match, but instead of their first string, they sent out their scrubs. The Athletics refused to play, and another "championship" series went undecided.

By 1868 the arrangement of matches between baseball clubs was an intensely formal procedure, as shown by this invitation offered to the Lowell Base Ball Club of Boston by the Wamsotta Base Ball Club of New Bedford.

"THE SMALLEST TOUCH MAY CAUSE THE BODY PAIN."

"O, UNEXPECTED STROKE, WORSE THAN OF DEATH."

The difficulties of fielding in the early days of baseball was one focus of Base Ball as Viewed by a Muffin, *a collection of cartoons considered to be baseball's first picture book. Muffins were the most inept players on any club, and S. Van Campen chose their perspective for his book, published in 1867.*

A few days after the Athletics-Atlantics muffin fiasco, the Excelsiors of Philadelphia met the Uniques of Brooklyn for what was billed as the "colored championship" of the United States. Apparently not allowed to play at Brooklyn's Union Grounds, the teams played on the nearby Satellite Grounds. The game was covered in the press, complete with quotations in dialect. Then as now, sport was conservative. The National Association was more concerned about welcoming new southern clubs to its fold than in integrating the "national game" racially. At the 1866 convention, the press noted that applause for erstwhile Confederates among its delegates "afforded ample proof of the truly conservative feeling which prevailed at the Convention."

The exclusion of black ballplayers from the highest levels of organized baseball was probably an informal—but rock-solid—policy. In 1867, while the states were ratifying the Fourteenth Amendment, the National Association unequivocally took a stand "against the admission of any club which may be composed of one or more colored persons" on the grounds that to admit "colored clubs" would lead to "some division of feeling, whereas, by excluding them no injury could result to anybody, and the possibility of any rupture being created on political grounds would be avoided." This delicate regard for feelings proved to be one of baseball's most enduring customs. The policy was reinforced in the late 1880s when Cap Anson refused to take the field against a Newark team that featured George Stovey, a fine black pitcher, and it was punctured only once or twice over the next few decades, until it was finally breached by Branch Rickey and Jackie Robinson in 1947.

The NA had also taken a stand against teams paying their players. But that didn't stop them. By the late 1860s more and more of the best clubs were—in one way or another—paying salaries. The first known pro was

Continued on page 76

Baseball on Campus

When baseball went to college, it went in a big way. The first intercollegiate ballgame was played on July 1, 1859, in Pittsfield, Massachusetts, under Massachusetts game rules. Amherst and Williams College went head to head in a 26-inning contest that Amherst won, 66–32. By 1866 Harvard had formed a ballclub under the more conservative New York rules: nine innings, nine players to a side.

The same year, Vassar formed the first women's team. "The public so far as it knew of our playing was shocked," said one member, "but we continued to play in spite of a censorious public."

When Amherst hosted Williams in the first intercollegiate baseball game, it was just half of a baseball-chess doubleheader. Amherst was presented with the game ball as a trophy for its win.

The 1870 Harvard baseball team (left) gave the Cincinnati Red Stockings a run for their money, but New England wasn't the only place where baseball on campus thrived. Spirited games could be found as far south as Emmittsburg, Maryland, home of Mount St. Mary's College (opposite).

In the 1860s and 1870s most college men's teams played local amateur clubs rather than other collegiate teams. In 1870 Harvard led the Cincinnati Red Stockings 17–12 before finally losing, and in 1873 and 1879 they beat the Boston Red Stockings.

Even if they didn't have the best players, college teams have always had the most enthusiastic fans. When Harvard faced the Boston Lowells in 1867, Henry Chadwick wrote that "the partizans on each side hissed nearly every decision of the umpire. The yells of derision, when errors were committed, were only equalled by the jeers of juvenile roughs in New York on similar occasions, and were entirely out of place as befitting an educated crowd." Some things never change.

In the 1860s Harvard gained a reputation for its ballplayers as well as its scholars. Henry Chadwick called an 1867 game between Harvard and the Lowell Club of Boston "the finest played game we ever witnessed in New England."

No longer just a city game, by 1866 baseball had cruised through New York state to Elmira, where the Hudson River Base Ball Club of Newburgh played before a good-sized crowd, both human and equine.

pitcher Jim Creighton, hired and paid by the Excelsiors in 1860. Creighton first appeared with the Niagara Club of Brooklyn in 1858. He was so effective against the neighboring Star Club the next year that they wooed him away. For the Stars, he beat the famed Excelsiors. The Excelsiors then induced Creighton to join them for the 1860 season. Creighton had a short but brilliant career that was based on the fact that he was baseball's first offensive pitcher. The rules in those days said: "The ball must be pitched, not jerked or thrown." To early rulemakers, "pitched" meant a specific underhand motion, the way horseshoes are pitched. A jerked ball was one pitched with a snap of the wrist. A thrown ball was one delivered overhand with the kind of arm motion pitchers use today. As early rulemakers envisioned it, the pitcher was supposed to toss the ball up so the batter could get it into play.

Although he was almost certainly jerking the ball, Creighton somehow got around the rules to deliver very fast pitches with excellent control. He was famous for his "speed ball." Creighton probably looked to batters of his day much as good fast-pitch softball pitchers look to batters today. He released the ball low, put a lot of steam on it and it rose all the way to the plate. If Candy Cummings is in the Hall of Fame for inventing the curve, Creighton should probably be there for inventing baseball's basic delivery: the fastball.

With Creighton, the Excelsior Club became one of the era's dominant teams. But the young star's career ended abruptly. On October 18, 1862, he suffered "a strain" slugging a home run and died a few days later at the age of 21.

Not long after Creighton's untimely death, toward the end of the Civil War, the Athletics paid first baseman Al Reach of Brooklyn's Eckfords $1,000 under the table to jump to Philadelphia. And in 1867 the great George

"ON THE FLY."

This Celebrated Brand of Natural Leaf Virgª Tobacco is manufactured Expressly for the BASE BALL CLUBS of AMERICA

Wright moved to Washington, D.C., where he played shortstop and captained the Nationals. Men like Creighton, Reach and Wright were paid directly—if quietly—for playing ball. Others, like many college athletes today, were given salaries for other kinds of work they never had to perform. The young Al Spalding, for example, was enticed to Chicago from his Rockford club by the offer of a vastly overpaid "job" as a grocer's clerk.

Players who moved from one team to another in those days were called "revolvers" or "shooting stars." They were the equivalents of free agents, selling their skill to the highest bidder. But for a long time, they couldn't sell those skills openly because of the policies of the National Association. Players and clubs had to cut their deals under the table. Everyone knew, for example, that George Wright was being paid by the Nationals, but the club felt compelled to list him as a "government clerk."

Things changed soon enough. George Wright joined his brother Harry with the Red Stockings in Cincinnati, and the professionals took charge of the sport. Baseball was growing up. ◐

Using baseball as an advertising tool became popular in the 1860s. This tobacco company label was a reminder that since 1858 only balls caught on the fly were counted as outs.

Candy Cummings

On a summer day in 1863, the flight of a clamshell on a Brooklyn beach turned a 14-year-old boy into baseball's all-time career wrecker. The curveball—the pitch that has dashed more major league dreams than any other—was born that day, the brainchild of Arthur Cummings.

Cummings watched as the clamshells he threw traced an arc through the air and wondered if he might be able to make a baseball do the same thing. So he bought a nickel ball and spent the better part of the next four years trying to turn his theory into practice. His desire to make the ball curve started out as a joke he wanted to play on his friends, with whom he had been playing three old cat and town ball. At first Cummings put himself through all sorts of gyrations, thinking that it was his windup that would make the ball curve. No luck. "Sometimes I thought I had it," he wrote, "and then maybe again in twenty-five tries I could not get the slightest curve."

In 1864 Cummings took his incipient pitch to boarding school in Fulton, New York, where his persistence amused some of his schoolmates and worried others. "The great wonder to me now is that I did not give up in disgust, for I had not one single word of encouragement in all that time, while my attempts were a standing joke among my friends," Cummings wrote in 1908. "I fear that some of them thought it was so preposterous that it was no joke, and that I should be carefully watched over."

After graduating, Cummings returned to Brooklyn, where even without a consistent curve he became the ace—and only—pitcher for the Star Juniors. Standing only 5′ 9″ and never weighing more than 120 pounds, Cummings pitched all 39 of his team's games and won 37. His performance caught the eye of Joseph Legett, an executive with the Excelsiors, Brooklyn's best amateur team. Cummings joined the Excelsiors and kept working on his curve. His big break came during a game against Harvard College in 1867. With the wind blowing in his face—a condition he discovered was favorable for curving—and some skeptics in the crowd, including a few physics professors, Cummings turned the Harvard hitters crimson.

Snapping his wrist—an illegal act—at the point of release in his underhand delivery, Cummings baffled the opposition. Archie Bush, Harvard's best player, "swung at the first curve ball I pitched, but he missed it by a foot," Cummings said. "I knew then that he was at my mercy. A surge of joy flooded over me that I shall never forget." The hitters got more frustrated and Cummings more delighted as the game wore on. "I felt like shouting out that I had made a ball curve; but I said not a word, and saw many a batter in that game throw down his stick in disgust. Every time I was successful I could scarcely keep from dancing from pure joy. The secret was mine."

In 1868 Cummings joined the Stars of Brooklyn, the self-proclaimed "championship team of the United States and Canada," and somewhere along the line picked up his nickname, "Candy," which back then meant "the best." For four years he was the Stars' primary pitcher, and his reputation grew. In 1870 no less an authority than Henry Chadwick, baseball's first great sportswriter, called him the best pitcher in the land. He made Chadwick look like a genius in 1871 when he held the New York Mutuals—a member of the newly formed National Association—to only three runs, an embarrassingly low output. Cummings became the most sought-after

Inventing the curve got Candy Cummings a spot in the Hall of Fame, but it didn't come without a price. He had to wear a glove on his pitching hand to prevent blisters and once broke his wrist throwing the pitch.

free agent around. With contracts being as loose as they were in the 1870s, he signed with three other clubs before finally deciding to play for the Mutuals, who got their money's worth. In 1872 the team went 34–20; Cummings was 33–20.

Players in the National Association moved around pretty freely, and 1873 found Cummings pitching for the Lord Baltimores with his customary success. He went 28–14, then moved to Philadelphia in 1874 and went 28–26, then moved to the Hartford Dark Blues in 1875, where he combined with a young Irishman named Tommy Bond to form one of baseball's first great starting rotations. Cummings won 35 and lost only 12 in 1875, and the following year the Dark Blues joined the new National League. Bond blossomed into the staff ace that season, but Cummings still went 16–8 with a 1.67 ERA, the league's third best, and his season had some true highlights.

In 1876 Cummings (back row, center) didn't pitch a game from May through August for Hartford. But when staff ace Tommy Bond (back row, second from right) had a fight with manager Bob Ferguson (front row, center), Cummings got the call and won 16 of 24 decisions to help Hartford finish third in the National League's inaugural season.

In his first start, he got St. Louis batters to pop out 24 times—21 times to the catcher; three he caught himself. And on September 9 he became the first player in the NL to pitch two complete-game wins in a doubleheader, beating Cincinnati 14–4 and 8–4.

But the workload took its toll. Playing in Cincinnati in 1877, his final season, he went 5–14 and took a beating from the fans and the press. "Seeing from 18 to 25 hits each day being piled up against Cummings' record is getting sickening," one newspaper reported. "His presence on the team is demoralizing. Unless this evil is remedied, the club on its return will not attract 100 people to the games. No change could be for the worse." At 28, Cummings had been throwing curveballs for 14 years, and just as he was the first player to experience the joy of the pitch, so too was he the first to experience its pain. Later that season, with his playing days behind him, he was named president of the short-lived International Association of Professional Base Ball Players, and soon Cummings was out of baseball altogether.

Other pitchers in Cummings' time had also been credited with throwing the first curveball, among them Phonnie Martin, Bobby Mathews, Fred Goldsmith and Joseph Mann. But in the 1890s the NL established a commission which concluded that Cummings deserved credit as the pitch's inventor. In 1908 he wrote an article for *Baseball Magazine* entitled, "How I Pitched the First Curve," in which he outlined the method for his maddening pitch. "I give the ball a sharp twist with the middle finger, which causes it to revolve with a swift rotary motion. The air also, for a limited space around it begins to revolve, making a great swirl, until there is enough pressure to force the ball out of true line." But Cummings' experience with the curve was much more emotional than scientific, and his reaction to his first successful curve was probably no different than that of the thousands of pitchers who followed. "The baseball came to have new meaning to me," he wrote. "It almost seemed to have life."

Cummings (left) honed his curve with the Brooklyn Stars from 1868 through 1871, and made hitters look bad in the process. "His opponents, not used to that sort of thing, often nearly broke their necks trying to reach after and hit the ball," wrote Al Spink.

CANDY CUMMINGS

Right-Handed Pitcher
National Association
New York Mutuals 1872
Lord Baltimores 1873
Philadelphia White Stockings 1874
Hartford Dark Blues 1875
National League
Hartford Dark Blues 1876
Cincinnati Red Stockings 1877
Hall of Fame 1939

GAMES	**246**
WINS	
Career	145
Season High	35
LOSSES	
Career	94
Season High	26
WINNING PERCENTAGE	
Career	.607
Season High	.745
INNINGS (NL only)	
Career	371⅔
Season High	216
ERA (NL only)	
Career	2.78
Season Low	1.67
COMPLETE GAMES (NL only)	
Career	40
Season High	24
SHUTOUTS (NL only)	
Career	5
Season High	5
STRIKEOUTS (NL only)	
Career	37
Season High	26
WALKS (NL only)	
Career	27
Season High	14

Combined NA and NL stats unless otherwise noted

C. M. McVey. R.F.   C. H. Gould. 1B.   Harry Wright. Capt & C.F.   G. Wright. S.S.   F. Waterman. 3d B.

A. J. Leonard. L.F.   D. Allison. C.   A. Brainard. P.   C. Sweasy. 2d B.

Cincinnati "Red Stockings."

Champions 1869.

Games won 57, lost 0.

The Wright Brothers

n 1867 the National Base Ball Club of Washington, D.C., toured what was then called "the West." Although they weren't the best of the eastern clubs, The Nationals demolished the opposition from Columbus, Ohio, to St. Louis, taking on the region's best teams and losing only a single game on their trip. It was a clear demonstration of the superiority of eastern baseball. One of their victims was the Cincinnati Base Ball Club, founded as a purely amateur organization in 1866. But the Ohioans learned from the defeat. For the 1868 season, they decided to hire some talent. With five eastern professionals on the roster, the 1868 Cincinnati Club was a powerhouse: clearly the best team in the West, and the equal of most in the East.

But Cincinnati still wasn't quite ready to play with the big boys. The Athletics of Philadelphia and the Atlantics of Brooklyn came west in 1868 and took the measure of the Cincinnatis, 20–13 and 31–7. Undaunted, the young club bravely undertook its own tour near the end of the season, the first time a western team had come east to meet the sport's top clubs. The Cincinnatis lost again to the Athletics and the Atlantics, as well as to the Olympics of Washington. But they beat their other opponents, including the New York Mutuals, who'd had a good enough season to be claiming the national championship. Cincinnati learned a lot from the top eastern teams and decided that they would teach the rest of the baseball world a thing or two.

Baseball's first openly professional club—the 1869 Cincinnati Red Stockings (opposite) —was also its most dominant. After beating everyone in the East and Midwest, they headed for San Francisco, where they pounded the Eagles, a local club, 35–4.

Mills. Zettlen. Pearce. Start. Smith. Ferguson. Crane. Pratt. Chapman.

THE ATLANTIC NINE, 1868.

In 1868 the Brooklyn Atlantics grabbed headlines and attracted crowds as the club toured cities across the Midwest. In June the Atlantics beat Detroit, 40–7, the Excelsiors of Chicago, 49–17, and the Forest Citys of Cleveland, 85–11.

On September 9, 1868, the club, led by president Aaron B. Champion, a prominent Cincinnati lawyer, decided to go fully professional. It built new grounds at the staggering cost of $20,000, found top-flight players, paid them salaries from March 15 to November 15 and—this was the revolutionary part—announced to the world exactly what they were doing.

To put this new professional team together, the club directors turned to a man they already knew well: the extraordinary Harry Wright. Wright had been born in Sheffield, England, in 1835. His father, Sam Wright, came to the United States a decade later to become the cricket pro at the St. George Cricket Club in New York. Harry was learning the English game from his father at roughly the same time that the Knickerbockers and their friends were developing the New York game of baseball. In the late 1850s Harry joined the Knickerbockers and played with them at the Elysian Fields. He was so good that he was chosen to represent New York in right field in the all-star Fashion Course Series of 1858.

Following in his father's footsteps, Wright moved to Cincinnati in 1865 as a cricket pro for the Union Cricket Club, earning $1,200 a year as a bowler and instructor. In 1867 the new Cincinnati Base Ball Club, which used the Union Grounds, hired him as a pitcher. He was a "cute" hurler, relying on control and his "dew drops"—which some call the game's first change-of-pace pitches. He was considered by one contemporary to have been "probably the trickiest pitcher in the United States." And he could hit, too. In a game against a team from Holt, Kentucky, he had seven home runs. But he had not yet dedicated himself to baseball. In September of 1868 Cincinnati took on the Active Club—the champions of Indiana. And they gave

Nelson, 3d B.;   Martin, R. F.;   Swandell, 2d B.;   Eggler, C. F.;
E. Mills, 1st B.;   Hatfield, S. S.;   C. Mills, C.;   Wolters, P.;   Patterson, L. F.

the Hoosiers a resounding 51–7 loss, even without their star pitcher, Wright, who was off playing cricket.

Nevertheless, once the Cincinnati Club directors made the decision to go all out in fielding a great team, Wright became serious and, with plenty of money in his pocket, went looking for "the best men procurable." His search took place in a new atmosphere. At its convention in November 1868, the National Association of Base Ball Players for the first time recognized the right of a team to hire players for pay. Professionalism in baseball had become legal.

But the Cincinnati Red Stockings were by no means the first professional club. While paying players a cut of the gate was technically against the rules through 1868, it was no secret that many teams—the Mutuals, the Atlantics, the Athletics, the Nationals, the Unions of Lansingburg, the Excelsiors of Chicago and the Red Stockings themselves —were doing it.

The Red Stockings probably weren't even the first club to put an entire team on salary. In 1869 the *Cincinnati Enquirer* noted that "the Mutuals have adopted the plan of paying each player a yearly stipend, in lieu of . . . dividing any proceeds . . . from gate-money. The sum so given is good and even generous wages."

But the Red Stockings *were* the first team to make no bones about their professionalism. They announced their intention more than a month before the National Association changed its rules. And they were about to demonstrate, as A. G. Spalding later said, "the superiority of an organization of ball players, chosen and trained and paid for the work they were engaged to do,

Championships were elusive designations before actual leagues formed and standings were kept, but the New York Mutuals laid claim to the somewhat mythical title of champions of the National Association of Base Ball Players in 1868. In early October the Mutes beat the Atlantics for the first time since 1863, 25–22, and then on October 26 they wrested the championship away from the Atlantics with a 28–17 win before 15,000 fans.

The Good Life

Paying a man wages to play a game for other people's amusement was a new idea in the 1870s. A few of the first salaried baseball players could live well on their earnings, but most of them worked at other jobs in the off-season — this comparison of wages and costs in the 1870s tells why.

Hotel room, per night **$2-$3**

Baseball ticket
Men **$.25**
Boys **$.15**
Women **free**

Cost of Living
Two-story house, furnished **$7,500**
House rental, per year **$300-$600**

Straw hat **$1.00**

Shirt, handmade **$1.75**
Suit **$2.50-$24**

Quart of ice cream **$.35**

Living Wages
The Cincinnati Red Stockings 1869

Harry Wright	**cf**	**$1,200**
George Wright	**ss**	**$1,400**
Asa Brainard	**p**	**$1,100**
Fred Waterman	**3b**	**$1,000**
Charlie Sweasy	**2b**	**$800**
Charlie Gould	**1b**	**$800**
Doug Allison	**c**	**$800**
Andy Leonard	**lf**	**$800**
Cal McVey	**rf**	**$800**
Dick Hurley	**sub**	**$600**
Average annual earning 1870		**$489**
Skilled craftsman		**$825**
Common laborer		**$475**

over any and all organizations brought together as amateurs for the simple purpose of playing ball for exercise and entertainment."

Offering the players salaries between $600 and $1,400, Wright managed to assemble a great team. The largest salaries on the team of course went to Harry Wright and his brother George. Asa Brainard, then 28, earned the third-highest salary on the team. Although he played on the Red Stockings of 1868, he had been a Knickerbocker and was one of the fastest pitchers around. Douglas Allison, the catcher; Charlie Gould, the first baseman; and Fred Waterman, the third baseman, had also played on the Red Stockings of the previous year. Andy Leonard, whom Wright signed to play left field, began his baseball career at the age of 13, playing for the Gothams of Newark, New Jersey. Leonard later played for the Buckeyes of Cincinnati, where Wright must have observed his talent. Charlie Sweasy was another Buckeye, signed to play second base for the Red Stockings. Cal McVey, who went on to an illustrious career with Boston and Chicago teams, was lured away from the Indianapolis Actives to fill the position in right field.

George Wright was—by far—the greatest star of this great team. Like his brother Harry, he'd started off playing cricket with their father, but in the early 1860s he moved to the growing American sport. He began his career with Harry on the Gothams, then "revolved" to the Nationals and the Unions of Morrisania before Harry enticed him to Cincinnati. During the 1869 season, George played in 52 of the 57 club matches. He batted .518, scored 339 runs and hit 59 homers—one of which was generally considered to be the longest ball ever hit.

And George wasn't just a slugger. "Slightly bowlegged à la Honus Wagner," as a later writer described him, he resembled Wagner in other ways as well. He was a speedy and daring baserunner who used a variety of slides. Most important, though, he revolutionized the way his position was played. Shortstops typically played "shallow," in front of the line between second and third. Because he had a strong and accurate arm, George could effectively operate from "deep" shortstop, which gave him much more range. He constantly amazed spectators with his ability to reach ground balls that looked as if they were going through to the outfield. He was also skilled at spearing line drives in either bare hand, and at making leaping grabs of shots over his head. Unlike the reserved Harry, George let his delight in the game show. "Whenever he would pull off one of those grand, unexpected plays that were so dazzlingly surprising," one writer remembered decades later, "his prominent teeth would gleam and glisten in an array of white molars that would put our own Teddy Roosevelt and his famed dentistry in the shadow."

Not that the other Red Stockings were shabby ballplayers. At least one opponent claimed that pitcher Brainard was already throwing curves. Other hurlers of the era could make the ball break in practice, but couldn't manage it in game situations because the rules forbade a wrist snap. How Brainard managed to obscure the quick twist of his own wrist remains a mystery. It is known, though, that he employed a "striding delivery" similar to a cricket bowler's, rather than the fixed-stance delivery many of his opponents used.

The key to the Red Stockings' success, though, was Harry Wright. As captain and manager, he trained his team in ways no other team had been trained before. He saw to it that they were fit, that they practiced in an or-

By beating the best teams in the East, the Red Stockings became the toast of Cincinnati. After news of their 4–2 win over the Mutuals reached Cincinnati's hometown "cranks," "salutes were fired, red lights burned and cheers were deafening," according to one scribe. "Joy reigned supreme." A proud fan could even sport one of baseball's first team buttons (below).

Pitcher Asa Brainard took center stage as the Red Stockings were immortalized in sheet music in 1869. Brainard was one of the team's true characters, a night owl and a hypochondriac with a baffling motion and an assortment of off-speed pitches.

ganized way and that they knew—as a team—what to do in certain situations. They had cut-off plays, and the fielders habitually backed each other up. This is all basic stuff today, but it was revolutionary in 1869.

Harry wasn't much of a hitter any more, and with Brainard on the team, he hardly pitched at all, stationing himself in the outfield. But he was the brains of the outfit. Although he demanded a lot of his men, he always treated them with respect, seldom raising his voice and never swearing.

But Wright had done more than put the Cincinnati team together; he had given serious thought to their uniforms, too, beginning a tradition that exists to this day. Ballplayers in the 1850s and 1860s generally wore their long trousers tied off at the bottom so they wouldn't flap. Harry decided that *his* club would wear knickerbockers, a style that had gone out 50 years before. The short, full pants gave his players more freedom of action. He contracted with a Mrs. Bertha Bertram to supply white flannel knee pants and shirts—an outfit remarkably similar to the uniforms worn today. Knickers, of course, require long stockings, and these were knitted for the team by the Truman sisters—daughters of a leading Cincinnati family—one of whom became the wife of pitcher Asa Brainard. The stockings these young ladies supplied were red and gave the team its name: the Cincinnati Red Stockings. And the players' striking uniforms impressed crowds almost as much as their skill, teamwork and athleticism. In San Francisco, one journalist wrote, "It is easy to see why they adopted the Red Stockings style of dress which shows their calves in all their magnitude and rotundity. Everyone of them has a large and well turned leg and everyone of them knows how to use it."

After three easy tune-ups at home, the Red Stockings hit the road to begin their famous tour. Within weeks, the team had become "the invincible 'Red Stockings' " and "our famous Red Stockings" in the Cincinnati press, proving the benefits of professionalism. In New York they beat the Mutuals in a heart-stopper by the unprecedented low score of 4–2, then followed up the next day by avenging the previous year's losses to the Atlantics by whipping the Brooklyn club, 32–10. They thoroughly drubbed the Athletics in Philadelphia and the Olympics in Washington before heading home with a 24–0 record.

Back in Cincinnati they kept winning until, on August 26, the Union Club of Lansingburg appeared at the ballpark. Better known as the Haymakers of Troy, this New York state club was a rough and rowdy squad—and a good one. In the sixth inning the score was tied at 17 when McVey came to the plate for Cincinnati. He tipped a ball foul, and the Haymaker catcher pretended that he'd caught it. The umpire disagreed. An argument ensued, and the Troy pitcher angrily ordered his team not continue the game. By this time, a riot was pending and the umpire climbed on a chair to announce to the crowd and players that he was forfeiting the game to Cincinnati.

Although the umpire awarded the game to the Red Stockings, the score was carried, even in their books, as a 17–17 tie, leading some to claim that Cincinnati had not won all its games in 1869. But during the winter of 1869–1870, the Troy club apologized to the Red Stockings and accepted the forfeit. Wright and his men may not have won the game on the field, but it was nevertheless their victory.

Three weeks after this close call, the Red Stockings took advantage of the newly opened transcontinental railway to head west. They were the first

Continued on page 92

The Haymakers of Troy, New York, inflicted the one blemish on the Red Stockings' otherwise spotless record in 1869—a 17–17 tie on August 27 in Cincinnati. The Reds actually won by forfeit when the Haymakers left the field after arguing a call by the umpire, but at least one account claims the Haymakers were ordered to find a way to leave by team owner John Morrissey, who was afraid of losing a $17,000 bet he'd placed on his team.

Cal McVey

Nearly a century before Bert Campaneris and Cesar Tovar made headlines by playing all nine positions in a single game, Cal McVey was defining baseball versatility. By the time he was 22, McVey had played every position but pitcher—he turned to that a few years later—and was even given the reins of a big-league club. But unlike many utility players who hung on in the majors mainly because of their versatility, McVey was a star-quality hitter and fielder who just happened to be able to play anywhere.

Born in Montrose, Iowa, McVey spent his teenage years in Indianapolis, and in 1867, at the tender age of 16, joined a local university team. He moved on to play for the Westerns and the Actives, two of Indianapolis' best teams, then caught the eye of Harry Wright, who signed the 18-year-old McVey to an $800 contract to play right field for the Cincinnati Red Stockings, baseball's first truly professional team. McVey, a well-muscled 5′ 9″ and 170 pounds, starred at catcher for the awesome Red Stockings, who barnstormed their way to an undefeated season. Two years later, McVey went along when Wright joined the Boston Red Stockings of the newly formed National Association and quickly became one of the league's best hitters. He tied for the NA lead with 65 hits and ranked second with a .419 batting average.

In 1873 he jumped to the Lord Baltimores, where he played eight positions while he managed the team to a third-place finish. The following year he was back in Boston, hitting .382 and leading the league in runs scored and hits, as the Red Stockings won their third of four straight pennants. In 1875 McVey—now playing mostly at first base—hit .352

as Boston laid waste to the NA in its final season, finishing 71–8.

In 1876 McVey changed the color of his stockings to white—along with Red Stockings stars Al Spalding, Ross Barnes and Deacon White—and joined Chicago of the new National League. He hit .347 batting third in the White Stockings' awesome lineup but added a new wrinkle as the team's number-two pitcher on a staff of two. McVey went 5–1 on the mound with a 1.52 ERA—even lower than Spalding's 1.75—as Chicago ran off with the NL's first pennant. But the White Stockings faltered in 1877, and a year later McVey became player-manager for Cincinnati, a team that had won just 24 games in the NL's first two seasons. Under McVey, Cincinnati improved to second place, just four games behind Boston. McVey's major league career ended after the 1879 season, in which Cincinnati finished fifth, and he took off for California, which he had first seen as a teenager on the Red Stockings' 1869 cross-country tour.

McVey spent the next ten years as a player and manager in California, and his long association with the game helped him get through some tough times. He lost his home and all his possessions in the 1906 San Francisco earthquake and was severely injured in a 30-foot fall in a Nevada mine in 1913. But both times McVey's baseball friends came through with moral and financial support.

Despite playing on four league champions and posting a .346 lifetime batting average, McVey never made the Hall of Fame because he fell short of its ten-year major league service requirement. But in 1968 he was elected to the Iowa Sports Hall of Fame.

Cal McVey was a great hitter no matter what league he played in. After a splendid career with Boston of the National Association, he joined Chicago of the National League in 1876 and had two six-hit games in a four-day span in July.

CAL McVEY

First Base, Outfield, Catcher
Cincinnati Red Stockings 1869–1870
National Association
Boston Red Stockings 1871–1872,
  1874–1875
Lord Baltimores 1873
National League
Chicago White Stockings 1876–1877
Cincinnati Red Stockings 1878–1879

GAMES	**527**
AT-BATS	**2,518**
BATTING AVERAGE	
Career	**.346**
Season High	**.419**
HITS	
Career	**870**
Season High	**138**
RUNS	
Career	**553**
Season High	**90**
DOUBLES (NL only)	
Career	**52**
Season High	**18**
TRIPLES (NL only)	
Career	**17**
Season High	**7**
HOME RUNS (NL only)	
Career	**3**
Season High	**2**
SLUGGING AVERAGE (NL only)	
Career	**.407**
Season High	**.455**
RUNS BATTED IN (NL only)	
Career	**172**
Season High	**55**

Combined NA and NL stats unless otherwise noted

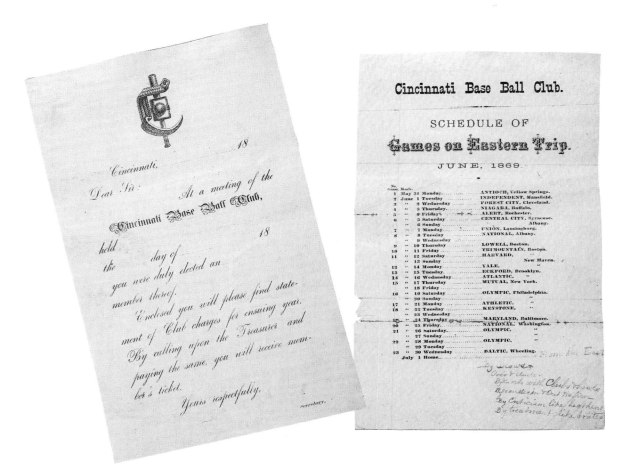

Harry Wright is credited with molding the Red Stockings into champions, but he would have been helpless without the wheeling and dealing of team owner Aaron Champion. Champion sold $13,000 worth of stock in the Cincinnati Base Ball Club—of which he was president—to club members in order to finance player purchases. The Red Stockings then took the East by storm, and when they returned, Champion declared that he would rather be president of the baseball club than president of the United States.

top team to reach the Pacific, and the first team of any kind to make a coast-to-coast tour. In San Francisco they played four baseball games and one cricket match—all of which they won. In Virginia City, Nevada, and Nebraska City and Omaha, Nebraska, they played a total of seven more games and won them all. The team was accompanied by Harry M. Millar, a reporter for the *Cincinnati Commercial,* who telegraphed game accounts back to his paper. Writers had accompanied touring teams before—Henry "Father" Chadwick had come west with the Washington Nationals in 1867—but no one had ever regularly filed game stories by telegraph.

Home again, they won their final few games, including victories over the touring Athletics and Mutuals. Over the course of the season, from early May to early November, the Red Stockings played 57 club matches and six more "picked nine games" against what amounted to all-star teams. The club logged just under 12,000 miles and played before more than 200,000 spectators. Cincinnati's share of gate receipts came to $29,726.26. Unfortunately, expenses came to $29,724.87, for a total profit of $1.39. Nevertheless, they went undefeated for the season, outscoring their club opponents 2,395 to 574—an average score of 42 to 10. They failed to score in only 63 *innings* all season.

When the 1870 season began, the Red Stockings picked up where they'd left off. They won 27 straight games before pulling into Brooklyn to meet the Atlantics on June 14. The Capitoline Grounds were packed with 9,000 "cranks" who had paid 50 cents each to see these two great teams go at each other. Despite the Red Stockings' great season the year before, the Atlantics had been acclaimed as what one writer

called "the figmentary champions" of 1869 because they were the best of the eastern teams.

Cincinnati jumped out to a 3–0 lead in the third, but by the top of the seventh, the Atlantics had come back to lead 4–3. The teams battled to a 5–5 tie at the end of the eighth. Neither team could score in the ninth. At that point, the Atlantics, following custom, declared the game a draw and headed for their clubhouse. But Harry Wright insisted that the rules said a game tied in the ninth had to be played to a conclusion. The Atlantics insisted just as forcefully that the game was over and that the Red Stockings had to accept a draw. Finally, the question was put to Henry Chadwick, chairman of the National Association's Rules Committee. Chadwick ruled in favor of the Red Stockings.

Cincinnati didn't score in the top of the tenth, but in the bottom of the inning, George Wright pulled the kind of heads-up play for which he was so well known—a play that is indirectly remembered today every time an umpire invokes the infield fly rule. The Atlantics were threatening, with men on first and second, when the batter popped up to short. Wright made as if to catch the ball, then quickly squatted to the ground and let the ball drop. He immediately trapped it, then threw to Waterman at third, who relayed to Sweasy at second for the double play on the runners, who had naturally been holding their bases. The Atlantic rally was squelched and the crowd—already wrung out with the tension of a well-played, low-scoring game—went wild over this bit of deception.

In the top of the 11th, the Red Stockings scored twice and seemed to be on the verge of extending their winning streak. Some spectators actually began to leave the grounds as the Atlantics came to bat. But Asa Brain-

When the Red Stockings opened the 1869 season with a 24–15 win over a team of local players, there was no brass band and no politician throwing out the first ball. But when they returned to Cincinnati undefeated after their tour against the East's finest teams, the red carpet was rolled out. They were presented with a 27-foot-long bat from a local lumber company (above) and were guests at a gala banquet filled with local dignitaries.

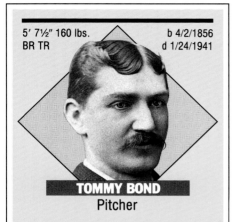

5' 7½" 160 lbs.
BR TR

b 4/2/1856
d 1/24/1941

TOMMY BOND
Pitcher

From 1877 to 1879, Tommy Bond set a standard that no pitcher will ever match: he earned at least 40 victories three seasons in a row. Pitching nearly every game for the Boston Red Stockings of the National League, Bond compiled records of 40–17, 40–19 and 43–19, and led Boston to two pennants and one second-place finish.

During those three iron-man seasons, the native of Granard, Ireland, led the league twice in wins, ERA and strikeouts, and three times in shutouts. Bond's reward for his unparalleled excellence? He became one of the earliest victims of the reserve clause, which club owners devised to keep players and hold down salaries—his pay dropped from $2,200 in 1879 to $1,500 in 1880.

In just ten seasons, the peripatetic Bond became one of the few players to play in four professional leagues. He started his career in 1874 with the Brooklyn Atlantics of the National Association, then played for the NL teams of Hartford, Boston and then Worcester, where he also managed for a short time. He closed out his playing career in 1884 with stops at Boston of the Union Association and Indianapolis of the American Association.

Known in his prime for "ruining" catchers with his underhand, cannonball delivery, Bond retired with a 234–163 record—and a worn-out arm. Back in Boston, he went to work at the city assessor's office and coached baseball at Harvard.

Victory cigars were the order of the day in Cincinnati in 1869, as the Red Stockings went undefeated and provided some of the first pro sports merchandising opportunities, like this cigar cutter.

ard, who had pitched so many innings over the past year and a half, gave up a base hit, wild-pitched the runner to third, then gave up a long hit to Joe Start. When left fielder Cal McVey leaned into the crowd to grab it, a spectator interfered with the play. By the time McVey threw the ball in, Start was on third and a run had scored. Atlantic captain Bob Ferguson then got a base hit to score Start, and the game was tied again, with a runner on first and one out.

All movement to the exits ceased. The Brooklyn crowd was almost out of control with excitement, and play had to be halted while order was restored. When the game resumed, Brainard induced the batter to hit the ball on the ground toward first baseman Charlie Gould, who promptly let it go through his legs. He chased it down, spotted the baserunner heading for third and uncorked a throw. The throw went wild, and the Atlantic runner kept going to score the winning run, giving his club an 8–7 victory and ending the Red Stockings' amazing streak of more than 90 consecutive wins.

From then on, the Red Stockings were not the same team—or maybe the rest of baseball was simply catching up to them. They lost five more games in 1870 and suddenly were no longer the dominant force in the sport. Attendance fell off, and relations soured between the team and the directors, who began to begrudge what they called the "enormous" salaries they were paying their men. The streak was over and—unable to earn its backers a profit—the great team passed out of existence after the 1870 season. The *Cincinnati Gazette* wrote that "the baseball mania has run its course. It has no future as a professional endeavor."

Despite the epitaph, professional baseball had only just begun. The Wright brothers, too, had only just begun their baseball careers. Harry left

for Boston, where he continued as one of the game's great organizational figures. His Boston teams, which included so many of the old Cincinnati players that they were also called the Red Stockings, won the professional National Association championship four times in a row, 1872 through 1875. Harry led Boston to two more championships in the early years of the new National League, then managed at Providence and Philadelphia until he retired in 1893, by which time the press was calling him the "Nestor" and the "Prince of Managers." He spent the last two years of his life on the National League payroll as chief of umpires.

Harry was treated with respect verging on veneration. After he died in 1895, Henry Chadwick wrote, "There is no questioning that Harry Wright was the father of professional ball playing. He was the most experienced, skillful and successful manager of a baseball team in the professional fraternity. His high integrity of character, his unassuming manner and his perfect knowledge of the game commanded the respect of every player who ever served under him."

George played for his brother's great Boston teams through 1878, but began to fade as a player in the late 1870s. Some believe that he had problems hitting the curveball, which became common about then. But it could also be that George was turning his attention elsewhere. He had started a sporting goods store in Boston in 1871. It hadn't really prospered, but he'd kept it going in the faith that he was headed in the right direction. In 1879 he took on a partner, Henry Ditson. Together, they formed Wright & Ditson, the sporting goods company that made George Wright a very wealthy man. That same year, George managed Providence to

The Red Stockings (above, left) stayed unbeaten well into the 1870 season, but other midwestern teams—like the Forest Citys of Cleveland (above, right)—also began to gain notice. When the New York Mutuals went on a midwestern tour that summer, they lost only twice—once to Cincinnati and once to the Forest Citys.

When the Red Stockings' amazing winning streak finally came to an end, it came in one of the finest, most pressure-packed games ever. After Cincinnati lost to the Atlantics, 8–7, in 11 innings at the Capitoline Grounds in Brooklyn, club president Aaron Champion sent a dispatch home: "The finest game ever played. Our boys did nobly, but fortune was against us . . . though beaten, not disgraced."

the National League pennant, and he remains the only manager in NL history to win a championship in his single year as manager. But George was always best known as a player, and he lived long enough to see himself elected to the new Baseball Hall of Fame in 1937. His brother Harry eventually joined him in 1953.

The Cincinnati Red Stockings, baseball's first legendary team, lasted only two years, but they established the whole idea of "professionalism"—of superior baseball through the teamwork of skilled, salaried players. And when the Red Stockings faded away in late 1870, they were not the only organization to sicken and die. The weak National Association of Base Ball Players didn't survive much longer, either. Professional baseball had become the norm among the best teams, and by the beginning of the 1871 season, a new, professional association—baseball's first major league—was established to accommodate the Red Stockings' legacy. ◖

*A week after the Atlantics ended Cincinnati's
unbeaten streak at 92 games, Brooklyn was
thrashed, 19–3, by the Philadelphia Athletics,
led by second baseman Al Reach (left) and
pitcher Dick McBride (right).*

HARRY WRIGHT

The first manager of an openly professional team, Harry Wright worked his players hard, but he was honest, fair and loyal to a fault. The affection his players felt for him, wrote The Sporting News, *"borders on adoration."*

Outfield
New York Knickerbockers 1858–1865
Cincinnati Red Stockings 1866–1870
National Association
Boston Red Stockings 1871–1875
National League
Boston Red Stockings 1876–1877
Manager
Boston Red Stockings 1876–1881
Providence Grays 1882–1883
Philadelphia Phillies 1884–1893
Hall of Fame 1953

GAMES	179
AT-BATS	851
BATTING AVERAGE	
Career	.263
Season High	.307
HITS	
Career	224
Season High	66
RUNS	
Career	182
Season High	57

NA stats only

NL Managerial Record

GAMES	
Career	1,917
Season High	155
WINS	
Career	1,042
Season High	87
LOSSES	
Career	848
Season High	73
WINNING PERCENTAGE	
Career	.551
Season High	.700

George Wright did everything but take tickets for the Cincinnati Red Stockings. He was the team's finest hitter and fielder, and sometimes entertained fans with pregame exhibitions of his juggling skill.

GEORGE WRIGHT

Shortstop
New York Gothams 1858–1863, 1866
Philadelphia Olympics 1865
Morrisania Unions 1866, 1868
Washington Nationals 1867
Cincinnati Red Stockings 1869–1870
National Association
Boston Red Stockings 1871–1875
National League
Boston Red Stockings 1876–1878,
  1880–1881
Providence Grays 1879, 1882
Manager 1879
Hall of Fame 1937

GAMES	**591**
AT-BATS	**2,894**
BATTING AVERAGE	
Career	**.303**
Season High	**.409**
HITS	
Career	**877**
Season High	**137**
RUNS	
Career	**663**
Season High	**105**
DOUBLES (NL only)	
Career	**54**
Season High	**18**
TRIPLES (NL only)	
Career	**20**
Season High	**10**
HOME RUNS (NL only)	
Career	**2**
Season High	**1**
RUNS BATTED IN (NL only)	
Career	**123**
Season High	**42**

Combined NA and NL stats unless otherwise noted

Growing Pains

In 1875 baseball's place on the American landscape was captured in watercolor and pencil by Thomas Eakins, one of America's greatest 19th-century painters. The work is entitled Baseball Players Practicing.

"The death of the National Association of Base Ball Players, which occurred in 1871, was expected, natural and painless. The organization had outlived its usefulness; it had fallen into evil ways; it had been in very bad company."

Albert Spalding

By the late 1860s, the National Association of Base Ball Players began to exhibit the worst traits of big city politics. The amateurs had been maneuvered out of power by what Henry Chadwick called "an unscrupulous clique of men hailing from the professional clubs." The last straw came during the NABBP convention of November 1870, when these back-room baseball politicos engineered the return of William Wansley, one of three Mutual players who had been banned for game throwing in 1865. The others, Thomas Devyr and Edward Duffy, had been reinstated in 1867 and 1869, respectively.

Outraged at being outmaneuvered, the amateurs broke with the National Association and founded a new organization pledged to upholding the best qualities of club baseball, the National Association of Amateur Base Ball Players. The professionals, too, decided to form their own group, the National Association of Professional Base Ball Players—with the emphasis, as Spalding wrote, on the word *professional*. The NABBP, eaten away with dissension, soon expired.

Few of those involved realized it, but the pros—unscrupulous and otherwise—already dominated the game. The Cincinnati Red Stockings had demonstrated the appeal of openly professional baseball. The new amateur association itself lasted only a year before it collapsed, leaving the professionals in charge of the sport.

The NAPBBP, called simply the National Association, was hastily put together by representatives of ten professional clubs meeting in New York City on the evening of March 17, 1871. To their credit, the founders worked out the first set of rules for a true national championship: each member club had to play every other team in a best-of-five series before November 1.

The club that won the most of these series—not necessarily the most games—would be named champion and would be allowed to fly a pennant during the following season.

Although this simple improvement excited much interest, in most other ways the new NAPBBP resembled its predecessor. Not only did the founders rather casually adopt the rules of the late National Association, they also referred to the new organization by the same name and continued to leave scheduling up to the individual teams—each of which could and did schedule lucrative games with clubs outside the association. And the new NA did little to restrict membership. To compete for the professional championship of the United States, all a club had to do was get up a $10 entry fee. Even at that, the Eckfords of Brooklyn—one of the original members—felt the cost was too high and didn't pony up until August, when it was too late to compete for the pennant.

Harry Wright represented his new Boston club and the Forest Citys of Rockford, Illinois, at the New York meeting. The other teams starting the first season of the first professional baseball association were the Athletics of Philadelphia, a Chicago club soon to be called the White Stockings, Cleveland's Forest City Club, the Mutuals of New York, Washington's Olympics, the Unions of Troy—they had just officially changed their name from the Unions of Lansingburg—and the Kekiongas of Fort Wayne, Indiana.

The Chicago team had been put together to challenge Cincinnati's formidable Red Stockings for 1871 and had beaten the fading Reds late in the previous season. Chicago managed to acquire pitcher George "the Charmer"

In 1870 the Chicago White Stockings (above) entered the pro ranks, and manager Tom Foley was sent out to raid other teams for high-priced talent. Levi Meyerle (front row, far left) was lured away from the Athletics for $1,500 a season but, in the fashion of the times, was back in Philadelphia in 1871 and back again in Chicago in 1874.

Revolvers

Baseball teams and leagues sprang up and folded unexpectedly in baseball's infancy, and players commonly jumped, or "revolved," from one team to another for a few dollars more. Contracts were not taken all that seriously, and team loyalty was less important to players than moving on to a better team and better rewards when the opportunity arose.

George Zettlein

1869-70	Brooklyn Atlantics
1871	Chicago White Stockings
1872	Troy (NY) Haymakers
1872	Brooklyn Eckfords
1873	Philadelphias
1874	Chicago White Stockings
1875	Philadelphias
1875	Chicago White Stockings
1876	Philadelphia Athletics

Doug Allison

1869-70	Cincinnati Red Stockings
1871	Washington Olympics
1872	Brooklyn Eckfords
1872	Troy (NY) Haymakers
1873	New York Mutuals
1873	Elizabeth (NJ) Resolutes
1874	New York Mutuals
1875-77	Hartford (CT) Dark Blues

Davy Force

1869-71	Washington Olympics
1872	Troy (NY) Haymakers
1872-73	Lord Baltimores
1874	Chicago White Stockings
1875-76	Philadelphia Athletics
1876	New York Mutuals
1877	St. Louis Brown Stockings
1878-79	Buffalo Bisons

Second baseman Sam Jackson of the Boston Red Stockings didn't have much to show for his 1871 season, as he hit just .195 in 15 games. But he did have this pin.

Zettlein, who had been the winning pitcher when the Brooklyn Atlantics shook the Red Stockings from their undefeated streak in 1870. They had also recruited powerful hitters Jimmy Wood and Fred Treacey, along with first baseman Bub McAtee, who had a reputation as one of the best defensive players in the country.

During most of the National Association's first season, the White Stockings looked as if they might snap up that new pennant. They were undefeated in association and non-association games when they pulled into New York to play the Mutuals at Cammeyer's Union Grounds in Brooklyn on June 5. This was a big game, and Mutual fans were ready: "Vast numbers," wrote an observer, "congregated on long porches of the clubhouse; on the beautiful sloping grass-covered banks along the side of the grounds and on the emerald-hued plots just outside of the fielders. The beautiful pagoda at the lower end of the grounds from the tall tapering flagstaff of which waved majestically the whip pennant of the Mutuals, and the newly erected stand, just at the right of the main entrance, were alive with beautiful ladies and gentlemen." The White Stockings were especially fashionable themselves, dressed in "cream white cap, shirt, knickers and hose, with string red ribbon and bow at the top of the stockings."

Inspired by this lovely scene, the Mutuals won, 8–5, but Chicago continued to play fine ball. By mid-September, the White Stockings' record was 17–8 against NA opponents, and they had won all three series they had completed. Boston, with a formidable lineup that included the Wright brothers, Ross Barnes, Cal McVey and Al Spalding, was also 3–0 in series contests, with a 15–9 overall record. The Athletics, at 17–9 overall, had won three series and lost one—to Boston. At the end of the month, Chicago played its

series with Boston, and when they took it, three games to one, the White Stockings looked to be in great shape to take the championship.

But Mrs. O'Leary's cow intervened. In early October, the great Chicago fire raged through the city, destroying the club's Lake Shore grounds, along with the team's equipment and elegant uniforms. Most of the players lost everything they owned. Not only did they miss games with Troy and Philadelphia, the team and its players were destitute. To add insult to injury, pitcher Zettlein was beaten up by a mob that took him for a looter when he was sorting through the rubble of his charred house.

The only course open to the poor White Stockings was to try to continue the season and bring in what money they could. Penniless, they begged a trip to New York, where they got a small stake from the proceeds of a couple of benefit games played on their behalf by the Mutuals and the Athletics. With this money, they moved on to Troy, where they won two games but took in very little cash because of the bad weather.

By this time, the championship committee had decreed that a single game between Chicago and the Athletics would settle the title for the season. The Red Stockings, who had won their series against Philadelphia, weren't happy about this, but their complaints to the A's-dominated committee fell on deaf ears. The White Stockings and Athletics headed for neutral turf in Brooklyn for their decisive game on October 30.

The Chicago players, still in desperate straits, were dressed in borrowed clothing: second baseman Ed Pinkham "wore a Mutual shirt, Mutual pants and red stockings," said one account. Mike Brannock, who had been picked up to play third base for the eastern trip, "wore a complete Mutual

In 1873 Philadelphia had two teams in the National Association—the Athletics, champions in 1871, and the upstart White Stockings, who had used higher salaries to snatch five players away from the Athletics, including 1871 batting champion Levi Meyerle. On October 12, with a 30–16 record, the White Stockings met the Athletics and scored six times in the ninth to win, 13–9 (above), but faltered down the stretch and were overtaken by Boston.

The Great Chicago Fire of 1871 left the Chicago White Stockings (left, with the Troy Haymakers) without a home field, uniforms and even caps. They played on, but in mismatched outfits, and finished second to Philadelphia in the first season of the National Association.

uniform, except the belt which was an Eckford." Outfielder Tom Foley "was attired in a complete Eckford suit," and Zettlein, " 'he of the big feet,' wore a huge shirt with a mammoth 'A' on the bosom." Shortstop Ed Duffy "appeared as a FlyAwayer." A few of the players wore regular baseball caps, others wore black hats and still others went bare-headed. "Many or most were broke," continued the account, "and they may have been actually hungry."

Led by veteran infielder Wes Fisler and pitcher Dick McBride, the well-fed Philadelphians surprised no one by winning the game and the first legitimate baseball championship. The White Stockings, devastated, withdrew from the National Association for 1872 and 1873 while their city rebuilt. They came back in 1874—with fashionable uniforms consisting of elegant Russian calfskin shoes with fancy tassels and a load of brand-new bats put in a bag inscribed with gold letters, "CHICAGO B.B.C. STUNNERS"—only to be burned out by another great blaze on July 15.

After winning the championship, the Athletics jubilantly hung their pennant in a Philadelphia tavern, attracting the wrath of Boston's Harry Wright, who felt that they should have displayed the flag in their club rooms. "To elevate the National Game," he said, "we must earn the respect of all; and now the Athletics are Champions—first legal and recognized Champion of the United States—they will be looked up to as the exponents of what is right and wrong in base ball." Wright never again had to worry about another team displaying the championship pennant inappropriately. His Red Stockings never lost another NA title.

After being engaged as manager of the new Boston club, Wright attracted a number of his old Cincinnati players to the team. His brother

First baseman Charlie Gould was no great shakes as a hitter —.254 lifetime—but he was better at the plate than he was in the dugout. In one season each as manager of New Haven in the NA and Cincinnati in the NL, Gould went 16–96.

JOE START
First Base

5' 9" 165 lbs.
BL TL

b 10/14/1842
d 3/27/1927

Throughout his 27-year playing career, Joe Start always seemed to come through in the clutch. In 1870 he was playing with the Brooklyn Atlantics in an extra-inning game against the Cincinnati Red Stockings, who were defending a winning streak of more than 90 games. In the bottom of the 11th, with the Atlantics down by two, Start tripled into the overflow crowd, kicking off the rally that led to an Atlantic victory.

The slugger—who hit .300 over 11 seasons in the NL—was even better in the field. In 1860, at 17, Start made his debut with the Brooklyn Enterprise. He was such a solid first baseman that he became one of the few early players to stay at one position throughout his career. Within ten years he earned the nickname "Old Reliable" for his sheer consistency in the field. One 1870 newspaper report described him as "very effective in taking in low balls, as well as those thrown over his head, and the hotter they come the more securely they appear to be held."

The left-hander is generally acknowledged as the earliest first baseman to play off the bag and narrow what had been a left-handed hitter's paradise —the huge gap between first and second. With his wider fielding range, Start was among the NL leaders in putouts and fielding percentage year after year. Had he played enough NL games to be considered among the record holders, his 10.9 putouts per game would rank first all-time.

George was the most important, but first baseman Charlie Gould and outfielder-catcher McVey were both among the game's best, too. Harry had also wooed and won Spalding and second baseman Barnes from Rockford. When McVey jumped to Baltimore for the 1873 season, Wright replaced him at catcher with Jim "Deacon" White from the Cleveland Forest Citys. And when McVey returned to the fold the following year, Harry had what came to be called "the Big Four" in place—Spalding, Barnes, McVey and White.

Spalding was the greatest pitcher of the era, very fast with fine control, and he won 207 games in five NA seasons. At 6' 1", 170 pounds, he was the biggest man on the team and a powerful hitter.

Barnes, who usually played second base, was a master of the fair-foul hit. In those days, a ball that landed fair but bounced foul before it passed first or third base was playable. Barnes could swat the ball into the dirt so that it landed in the playing field but skidded off toward the bench or into the crowd, and he'd often take extra bases before the infielder could retrieve it. Boston fans loved it, and they'd shout "Fair foul, Ross!" when he stepped up to the plate.

McVey and White were less spectacular but no less valuable. They were both "vigorous" batters and excellent defensive performers at a variety of positions. The Boston team was solid from the start, but shortstop George Wright—probably the best all-around player in baseball during the early 1870s—was in and out of the lineup with injuries throughout the 1871 season. Otherwise, Boston might well have won the first NA championship, instead of just the next four.

Of course, the Red Stockings had no monopoly on fine players. Most of the other old Cincinnati Red Stockings were still in action elsewhere in the

Continued on page 110

Al Reach

Al Reach's career in baseball was a classic rags-to-riches story. The son of poor English emigrants, he made his fortune in the sport that became the national pastime of his adopted land.

Shortly after his birth in 1840, Reach's parents emigrated from London to New York. The family struggled to make ends meet; as a young boy Reach sold newspapers on the streets of Brooklyn. He was a natural athlete who learned to play cricket with his father but preferred the fledgling American game of baseball. At 15 he joined the newly formed Brooklyn Eckfords as a second baseman.

Reach was a skilled fielder and baserunner, but it was the left-hander's bat that brought him fame. In 1862 the Eckfords became one of the first teams to play in an enclosed ballpark and to charge admission—as high as 50 cents a head on Opening Day. Crowds numbered in the thousands, and the big draw was the hard-hitting Reach.

Baseball in the early 1860s was still officially an amateur sport. But everyone knew that the best teams competed for talented players with promises of under-the-counter cash or offers of well-paying jobs from local businessmen. Teams in several cities bid for Reach; in 1865 he joined the Philadelphia Athletics for $25 a week, becoming baseball's first aboveboard professional.

Reach remained with the Athletics for 11 years. The Philadelphia team was a charter member of the National Association and captured the first league championship in 1871; Reach, who batted .348 that year, was named to one of baseball's first all-star teams, which was compiled by a newspaper, the *New York Clipper*. During his final two years as a player—1874 and 1875—he also managed the Philadelphia team, guiding it to consecutive winning seasons.

After his retirement he opened a cigar store in Philadelphia that became a hangout for sports fans and evolved into a company that manufactured and sold sports equipment. In partnership with Benjamin Shibe, the inventor of the cork-center baseball, Reach's firm pioneered methods of mass production and mail-order sales through catalogs. In 1883 he began publishing *Reach's Official Baseball Guide,* an annual report that fed the fans' growing appetite for reliable statistics.

At the end of the decade Reach sold his firm to his major competitor, A.G. Spalding & Bros., to create a virtual monopoly that dominated the sporting goods industry in America. But the two companies continued to operate under their old names, with Reach's name on the official statistical guide for the American League and Spalding's name on the National League guide. Spalding's Philadelphia plant manufactured all official league baseballs, but those used in the American League still bore the name of A. J. Reach.

While his business ventures made him a millionaire, Reach never lost touch with the game itself. In 1883 he joined other investors to bring an NL team—dubbed the Phillies—to Philadelphia. Reach served as team president until 1902. During his tenure, the Phillies built the finest park in the league, a facility that held 20,000; when this burned down in 1894, baseball's first steel stadium, Baker Bowl, was erected on the same site.

In 1907 Reach served on the Mills Commission, which gave its stamp of approval to the popular myth that Abner Doubleday invented baseball in Cooperstown, New York, in 1839.

AL REACH

Outfield, Second Base
Brooklyn Eckfords 1861–1864
Philadelphia Athletics 1865–1870
National Association
Philadelphia Athletics 1871–1875

GAMES	**81**
AT-BATS	**389**
BATTING AVERAGE	
Career	**.252**
Season High	**.348**
HITS	
Career	**98**
Season High	**47**
RUNS	
Career	**89**
Season High	**43**
NA stats only	

Sometimes a shift in position in the field can affect a player at the plate as well, and Al Reach was an extreme example. Reach batted .348 as a second baseman for the Philadelphia Athletics in 1871, then was switched to the outfield in 1872 and hit .191.

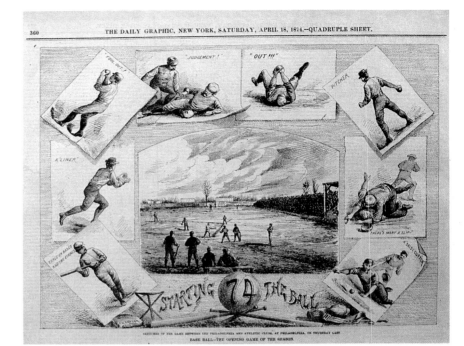

By 1874 Opening Day was a media event, so the New York Daily Graphic *reported on the opener between Philadelphia's crosstown rivals, the Athletics and the White Stockings. Behind the pitching of Dick McBride, the Athletics won, 14–5.*

For cranks not quite ready to take the field, baseball could be played in the parlor with board games like this one published by J. H. Singer. By this game's rules, three fouls were an out, but in organized baseball no such rule ever existed.

NA. In that first year, the Olympics of Washington picked up most of those players Wright didn't: third baseman Fred Waterman, catcher Doug Allison, second baseman-outfielder Andy Leonard and pitcher Asa Brainard.

These two teams, both loaded with members of that famous undefeated Cincinnati club, opened the first National Association season against each other. Brainard promptly set a record that still stands: he walked 17 batters. He may not have been the pitcher he was in 1869, but the numbers he ran up in this first game of the season were deceiving. Even in the opinion of one Boston paper, the umpire, a Mr. H. A. Dobson, "called balls and strikes too closely thus abridging the pleasure of the game." By this, the paper didn't mean that Dobson had too small a strike zone, but that he called every pitch that wasn't hit either a ball or a strike, which just wasn't done in those days —a holdover from the days when a pitcher's job was simply to let the batter get the ball in play.

Other pitchers were making names for themselves in more positive ways. Candy Cummings may or may not have invented the curveball, as he later claimed, but he was using it to good effect against mystified hitters. He won 124 games and lost 72 in four years with four different NA clubs. Bobby Mathews could make the ball break, too. He's sometimes called the father of the spitball. In the National Association, he won 132 games and lost 111, mostly for the Mutuals, then went on to win 166 and lose 138 in the National League and later in the American Association: 298 total victories in 15 seasons. Dick McBride was another great hurler of the era, compiling 152 wins against 76 losses in five seasons with the Philadelphia Athletics.

But these pitchers, as good as they were, didn't have the benefit of Boston's disciplined teamwork and Harry Wright's guidance. The Red

Stockings were simply supreme. Many baseball historians believe that they were *too* good—that they were so much better than the rest of the NA that the lack of balance turned off potential ticket buyers and caused many teams to fold. It's true that membership in the NA was extremely unstable. Some two dozen clubs joined the association during its five years of existence. Ten stayed for a single year, and only three—Boston, the Mutuals and the Athletics—competed all five seasons. But the league's instability had more to do with other teams' unrealistic expectations and poor financial management than with Boston's dominance. The Red Stockings, like the Yankees a half century later, drew well on the road—so well that Wright could demand an unusually large slice of road-trip gate receipts. In fact, the Red Stockings' financial success not only gave them more staying power, their popularity helped to carry weaker teams in other NA cities.

Nonetheless, Harry Wright, among others, urged the National Association to set higher standards for teams that wanted to enter championship play, including being in a city big enough to support the well-paid players necessary for top-class ball. These men wanted to avoid the embarrassment and inconvenience of having so many clubs joining the association, dropping out before the season was over and disrupting schedules. But the NA never moved on the issue. Teams continued to join the association, pay their dues, play a few games, collapse, re-form and try again.

Instability hurt the National Association's image, but it was far from the organization's biggest problem. Public confidence was profoundly shaken by the corruption that had taken hold in the professional association. In 1874 the *New York Herald* ran a tribute to the Red Stockings, saying that: "above all, they invariably play to win. The latter cannot be said of all the professional

The Independents of Mansfield were just one in a collection of fine teams in Ohio in the 1860s. Led by catcher John Clapp (second from left), the Independents were strong enough to attract the Boston Red Stockings to Mansfield in 1868 and 1869. Why the Independents are all smoking cigars in this photo is anybody's guess.

Players and owners were making money off baseball in the 1870s, and it wasn't long before others got in on the act. Printers began using the game as a subject for artwork (above), which was then sold for use on items such as cigar boxes and tobacco pouches.

nines now contesting for the championship. Indeed to such a low ebb have the morals of so many professional players descended that no man can now witness a game between many of the clubs and be sure that both sides are striving to win. Gamblers buy up one or more players to lose a game and it is lost."

Gambling was running the National Association straight into the gutter. In some cities, baseball was essentially run by gamblers for gamblers. Several teams habitually traveled with high rollers in their parties. The situation seemed to get worse each year. Talk of "sure thing" gamblers arranging the outcome of games was open and constant. In 1875 the *Brooklyn Eagle* even published a lineup, complete with subs, of "rogue" players who were assumed to be on the take—a sort of cheat's all-star team. Nobody sued.

Nineteenth-century "cranks," as fans were called, weren't stupid. They weren't interested in paying money to watch a game whose outcome had been arranged for the profit of bettors. They steered clear of some ballparks: the press of the day noted that the Philadelphia Phillies lost $3,000 in 1875. Attendance was down because the public never knew when the Phils were playing to win and when they weren't.

In some cities, gamblers virtually took over the stands, and there was so much foul language and rowdyism that gentlemen and their ladies preferred to take their custom elsewhere. Crowds in St. Louis and Philadelphia were especially tough, often menacing visiting players on the field after the game was over. Spalding was once hit in the head by a stone tossed at him in the City of Brotherly Love, and the Red Stockings eventually announced that they would play no more games there without police protection.

This state of affairs infuriated men like Harry Wright and journalist Henry Chadwick, who understood that the future of professional baseball depended on fans being entertained by skilled athletes engaged in honest competition. In Boston, the club went to great lengths to keep the game respectable—and profitable. Their park was one of very few in which no gambling at all was allowed, and they even installed a sign in the stands reminding patrons, "Don't dispute the umpire."

Despite efforts in Boston and a few other towns, it was clear by the end of the 1875 season that little could be done to clean things up under the National Association's weak rule. The game on the field—when it was played straight—had improved during the NA's life span. Players were making fewer and fewer errors, and pitchers were becoming more skilled. But the National Association was failing in its most important role: the protection and promotion of professional baseball as a profitable endeavor. The NA provided no central authority to deal with dishonest players or clubs. And few of the men involved even recognized the need for such an authority.

A few months after the close of the National Association's 1875 season, a group of businessmen established a new structure for professional baseball. They dropped the weak clubs from smaller towns and granted "territorial rights" to member clubs, thereby creating for themselves a monopoly that they hoped would lead to honesty, stability—and profits. They called their new organization the National League. ✸

The Boston Red Stockings made a mockery of the National Association pennant chase in 1875, leaving the second-place Philadelphia Athletics in their wake. Boston (both rows, right half) had its entire championship team back from the year before, while the Athletics (above, both rows, left half) obtained shortstop Davy Force from Chicago and introduced a whole new outfield. They went 53–20, but still finished 15 games behind Boston.

Bobby Mathews

Known as "Little Bobby"—he stood under 5′ 6″ and weighed no more than 140 pounds—Mathews was the prototype of the thinking man's pitcher. Since he couldn't overpower batters, the slight right-hander learned to outsmart them. One 19th-century writer called him "without doubt the most versatile boxman of his day."

Mathews first attracted attention as a 17-year-old amateur in 1869, when he pitched his hometown Baltimore team, the Maryland Juniors, to a 21–16 victory over the highly regarded Brooklyn Eckfords. Three years later, when the National Association of Professional Base Ball Players was organized, he signed with the Fort Wayne, Indiana, Kekiongas. In his professional debut, against a Cleveland team noted for its hitting, Mathews pitched a five-hit shutout—the lowest-scoring game recorded in the league that year.

Mathews played during the underhand era; there were restrictions on how high a pitcher could raise his arm when delivering the ball to the plate. He was expected to put the ball into play, not to strike the batter out, and the batter could even stipulate whether he wanted a high or low pitch. But Mathews stifled batters with a varied repertoire of pitches and deliveries, "hardly ever using the same delivery twice," according to one account. A fierce competitor with an innovative baseball mind, he was one of the first pitchers to use an underhand curve effectively. And he was credited with throwing the first spitball, a pitch that was not declared illegal until 1920. Because of the pitcher's innovations, one writer of the period said Mathews "occupied the spotlight of the baseball stage for fourteen years."

But during Mathews' time, the National Association's brief existence was marked by constant turmoil. Teams went out of business in midseason and players jumped from city to city in search of the best deal. In his five years in the NA, Mathews pitched for three teams. From 1873 through 1875 Mathews pitched for the New York Mutuals, the league's weakest hitting team, yet he won 100 games for them. In 1874 he pitched *all* of New York's 65 games and won 42 of them.

When the NA disbanded, the Mutuals became members of the new National League. An enterprising New York gambler offered Mathews $200 a game to let opposing teams win; the pitcher promptly reported the offer to William Hulbert, the most powerful man in the league, and helped to establish a new standard of honesty for professional baseball.

Unfortunately, the Mutuals failed to finish out the 1876 season, and over the next six years Mathews bounced around the country, playing for six different teams with little success. In 1883, when he was 31 years old, he landed with the Philadelphia Athletics of the American Association, and staged an amazing comeback. Relying mainly on control and his ability to outguess batters, he won 30 games and led the Athletics to the league championship in his first year. He followed that with two more 30-win seasons; in 1884 he struck out 16 batters in one game; the following year he averaged six strikeouts a game. By 1886 Mathews began to have trouble with his arm, and his pitching days were over. When he retired in 1887, Mathews had more victories—306—than any other active major league pitcher.

Bobby Mathews' baseball travels took him from the East Coast to the West Coast and back again. Best known for his stints with the New York Mutuals and the Philadelphia Athletics, Mathews struck out 12 in his 1880 debut with the San Francisco Stars.

BOBBY MATHEWS

Right-Handed Pitcher
Maryland Juniors 1868
Maryland Seniors 1869–1870
National Association
Fort Wayne Kekiongas 1871
Lord Baltimores 1872
New York Mutuals 1873–1875
National League
New York Mutuals 1876
Cincinnati Red Stockings 1877
Providence Grays 1879, 1881
Boston Red Stockings 1881–1882
International Association
Columbus Buckeyes 1877
Lynn Live Oaks 1878
American Association
Philadelphia Athletics 1883–1887

GAMES	600

WINS	
Career	306
Season High	42

LOSSES	
Career	262
Season High	38

WINNING PERCENTAGE	
Career	.539
Season High	.698

INNINGS (NL, AA only)	
Career	2,734⅓
Season High	516

ERA (NL, AA only)	
Career	3.00
Season Low	2.29

COMPLETE GAMES (NL, AA only)	
Career	289
Season High	55

STRIKEOUTS (NL, AA only)	
Career	1,199
Season High	286

Combined NA, NL, IA and AA stats unless otherwise noted

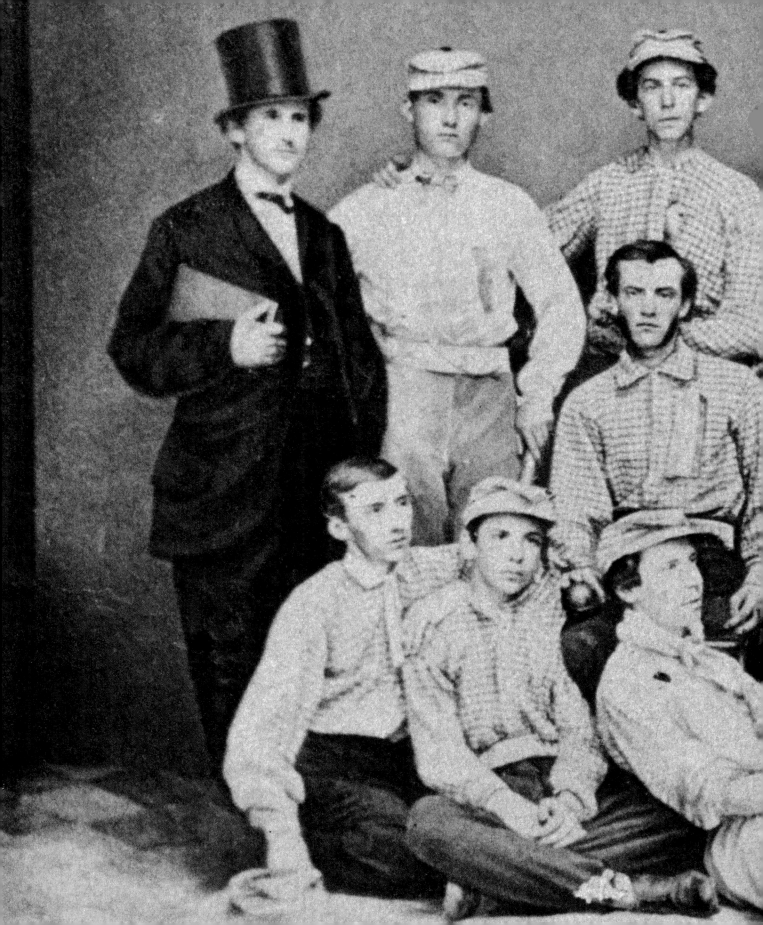

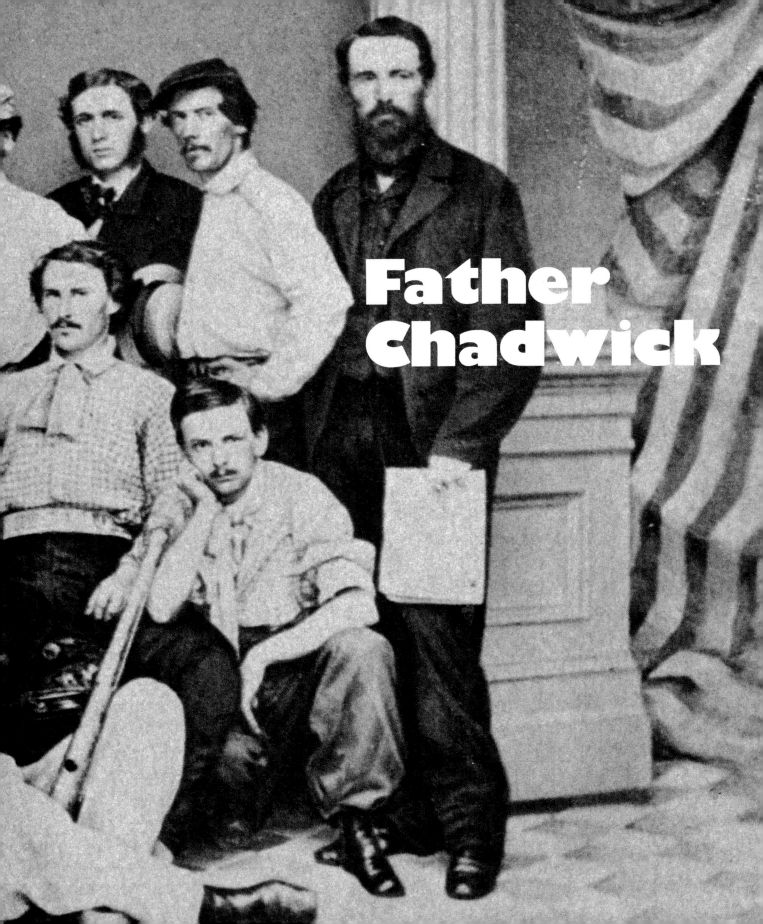

Father Chadwick

Henry Chadwick wrote about baseball for nearly 50 years, promoting and protecting the game through its infancy and into its adolescence. He worked into his eighties and attributed his longevity to his penchant for taking Turkish baths.

Sportswriters rarely pose with ballclubs, but then there's never really been a sportswriter like Henry Chadwick (preceding page, back row, far right, posing with the Resolutes of Brooklyn). This photo was taken in 1864, the year Chadwick began writing for the New York Herald *and five years after he invented the box score.*

My dear Sir," Henry Chadwick wrote in a 1906 form letter to ballclub officials. "I have to write an article this week on 'Irish Ball Players in America,' and I desire the names of all the players on your club team, who are of Irish birth or parentage and their general occupation; also whether they were college players, and their position in the ranks; whether Managers, Captains or players generally. Of course, I need this information as soon as possible." This was a baseball legend at work: the man known as "the Dean of Baseball Writers." And yet here he was hacking away as thousands of other sportswriters through the years have had to do—working up a silly story, on a deadline, in a hurry. Henry Chadwick may have a plaque on the wall at Cooperstown, but he was first and foremost a journalist who scrambled all his life to scratch out a living with his pen.

Chadwick virtually invented sportswriting as an occupation. By the time he wrote his letter asking for information on Irish ballplayers, he'd been covering baseball for half a century. He'd attacked its enemies, applauded its advances, encouraged its growth and instructed its fans. As a member of various rules committees, he'd had a strong hand in developing it from a simple recreation to a complex professional sport. And although it especially suited the bearded, dignified old man in his eighties, he'd long since earned the title by which he's still remembered. To baseball fans, Father Chadwick is as proper a name as Babe Ruth.

Chadwick was born in England and came to the United States with his parents in 1837 when he was 12 or 13. His father had been a journalist in the old country; his older brother Edwin, who stayed behind, was knighted for his work in designing sanitary sewage systems for London.

Baseball's two fathers—and two of its first lovers of statistics—appeared in the same photograph in 1863. Chadwick (middle row, far right) appeared with the St. George's Cricket Club while covering the sport for the New York Clipper, *while Harry Wright (bottom row, far right) was one of the club's star players.*

Young Henry began his working life as a piano teacher, but printer's ink flowed in his veins, and he turned to journalism in his mid-twenties. Covering baseball came later. The story goes that he took the ferry to New Jersey one day in the mid-1850s to watch a cricket match at the Elysian Fields. While he was there, he saw a baseball game in progress and recognized that it could become a more popular sport in the United States than cricket. He felt so strongly that the game should be publicized that he trudged around to every paper in the metropolitan area, offering to submit reports of intraclub match games without charging for his services. Even at that, only *The New York Times* accepted his offer, with the proviso that he make his reports as short as possible.

It's a nice story, but it's not true. Chadwick had been aware of the New York game almost from the start. He played shortstop with the Knickerbockers and their friends, qualifying as a true pioneer of the game. "The first base-ball match we ever played in," he wrote almost 30 years later, "was at the Elysian Fields in the fall of 1847."

"It was some years after that," he continued, "and after we had been reporting cricket for several seasons, that we took up base-ball, getting interested in it and seeing what a lever it would be to lift Americans into a love of outdoor sports." Chadwick, a proper Victorian, believed firmly in the physical and moral benefits of strenuous outdoor exercise. This is why, in later years, he was so bitterly disappointed at the gambling and game throwing that was rampant during the 1860s and 1870s. And it was why he turned on the players of the 1880s and 1890s, who he thought led dissolute and unregulated lives, squandering their talent and demeaning their sport.

There wasn't a whole lot published about baseball in the 1870s that did not flow from Chadwick's pen. Included in his responsibilities were the editorships of DeWitt's Baseball Guide *and* Beadle's Dime Base-Ball Player. *In his spare time he led a crusade to end gambling at ballparks.*

From the beginning, Chadwick threw himself into every aspect of the sport. He pushed for the conventions that established the original National Association, amateur baseball's first organization. He chaired the NA's rules committee. He quickly became the game's outstanding chronicler—and he was an official and a promoter to boot. By the end of the 1850s Henry Chadwick had clearly hitched his wagon to the star of the new American sport, and ten years later he was already being called "Father."

Al Spink, who founded *The Sporting News,* first saw Chadwick at a ballgame in Brooklyn in 1870. Before the game, he saw a tall man carrying a huge book under his arm, whom the players and everyone else treated with great respect.

"Who is he, this dignitary?" Spink asked.

"That's Chadwick," said a player, "the only man living who knows how to keep the score of a ball game. He can even tell you how well I hit the ball in a game played last year."

Either Spink or the player overstated the matter: by 1870 any number of reporters were regularly keeping scorecards—many of them using symbols suggested by Chadwick in *DeWitt's Baseball Guide,* which he edited from 1869 through 1880. Chadwick, though, had been among the first to keep detailed score sheets and is remembered to this day as the inventor of the newspaper box score, that masterpiece of concentrated communication.

In fact, Chadwick was one of the very first to fall under the spell of the game's statistics. His writings, a contemporary said, "had to do largely with statistics and itemized detail." But perhaps that was because Chadwick recognized right away that well-kept records could indicate the value of a player to his team more accurately than merely watching him perform.

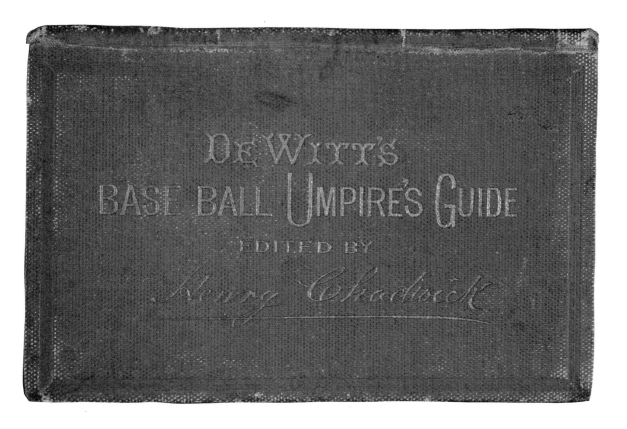

But Chadwick wasn't consumed by numbers. He paid close attention to the game on the field, too. Although baseball today is the most traditional of sports, it was anything but that during the 19th century. From the very start, the rules were constantly being adjusted to meet the increasing skill and inventiveness of the players. Most of those changes came straight from the pen of Chadwick himself. Every year he'd gather suggestions from players, captains and club officials, then he'd carefully study "the practical working of each rule," before presenting his proposed changes to the playing public in his *New York Clipper* column. Most were accepted. Chadwick was so identified with the new rules that at the opening of each season, he would umpire a practice game for the Atlantic Club at the Capitoline Grounds in Brooklyn, so that "the players get from him a correct interpretation of the amended rules."

When he showed up in April 1874 at "the Cap," as the ballfield was known, another baseball writer was there to watch the performance and described how Father counted "wides," or balls, by "passing a penny from one hand to the other." After the game Chadwick confided why he only umpired practice matches: "He says he is not fit to act as an umpire, as he gets too interested in the play; and, besides, he is altogether too nervous a man to act in a position requiring so much calmness and nerve." And yet this is the man who, in front of a howling crowd, coolly decided that extra innings had to be played in the game in which the Atlantics finally broke the Cincinnati Red Stockings' long winning streak.

By the mid-1870s, Chadwick had been the primary rulemaker for so long that he felt that his *Clipper* rules were virtually official. But he was rudely and publicly disabused of this notion. After the 1873 season, he began to agitate for a "right short-stop": "The base ball field as at present placed is what

Continued on page 124

Chadwick had a great deal of respect for the job of umpire, and edited baseball's first umpires' guide. He wrote that upon the umpire's "manly, fearless, and impartial conduct in a match mainly depends the pleasure that all, more or less, will derive from it."

The Birth of Sportswriting

From the 1850s through the 1870s, baseball traditions were being made, not obeyed, and the game was molded as much by weekend amateurs as by the few players who made their living on the field. Likewise, sportswriting was in its infancy, dominated by men without bylines, groping for a new language to describe a new game. The game of "Base Ball" described below was in reality the New England variant, known as the Massachusetts game.

EXCITING GAME OF BASE BALL —The second trial game of Base Ball took place on the Boston Common, Wednesday morning, May 14, between the Olympics and the Green Mountain Boys. The game was one hundred ins, and after three hours of exciting and hard playing, it was won by the Olimpics, merely by two, the Green Mountain Boys counting 98 tallies. The above match was witnessed by a very large assemblage, who seemed to take a great interest in it.

New York Clipper,
May 24, 1856

Before professional leagues, local pickup games could still make the papers. Consider this account of the Olympic Theatre versus the Fifth Avenue Theatre in "the first match ever played exclusively by actors."

Mr. Sol Smith, Jr, in the centre field particularly distinguished himself. The alarmingly wild and reckless manner with which he "went to work" with the "fell purpose" of accomplishing nothing whatever was something unprecedented in the annals of baseball playing.

Mr. C.K. Fox, in the use of the bat, evinced a delicate tenderness. Mr. J.J. Wallace, as a runnist, excelled himself by finding more new bases than any player we have ever seen.

New York Clipper,
1866

Baseball was not always a summer sport. Teams played games well into November, and when it got too cold, they put on skates and played on ice.

The Fultons disposed of their opponents for a single, and then went in with 18 runs to get to win. Ordinarily, this lead would have insured a victory for the Eckfords; but baseball on ice is a very slippery game, and twice as uncertain as it is in the field.

Mr. Wilson umpired the game very satisfactorily to all parties. The umpire's position on ice games is not a desirable one; but it has one advantage, he is obliged to take things coolly.

Sunday Mercury,
1868

Hit and run baseball was the rule, not raw power, and brilliant fielding—bare-handed, of course—brought crowds to their feet. The Boston Red Stockings and the Philadelphia Athletics put on a virtual fielding clinic when they met in the mid-1870s.

Schafer did a brilliant thing on the next inning by running down the field to take Batten's fly, and then throwing handsomely to O'Rourke in time to catch Sutton off and secure double play. Two artistic double plays by George Wright, Barnes and O'Rourke marked the fifth and sixth innings, and drew forth applause, which was only exceeded by that which followed a magnificent single-handed running fly catch by Leonard—the best individual play of the game.

Boston Herald,
1874

Poor play was common, but that doesn't mean the press had to like it. The acerbic sports columnists of today have nothing on their predecessors.

We would advise a meeting of the Athletic Club, and request the resignation of Schuylkill Ferguson, queer Spering, and 'umble Reach.

The three have proved their incompetency.

They are no more fit to manage the Athletic Club, than we are to sail a seventy-four.

Ferguson does not know one base from another. Spering was ever "queer," and Reach is too 'umble!

The Bostons were travel worn and tired, and yet they go in with solid, old, gallant Yankee pluck, and lick the Athletics out of their stockings!

Out with them! Throw them out on their ears on the sidewalk!

Philadelphia Press,
May 21, 1874

On June 3, 1874, the Boston Red Stockings beat the Chicago White Stockings, but a reporter from the Windy City expressed optimism about the next day's game.

The closeness of yesterday's score demonstrated that the Whites are a good team, and on Saturday it is confidently expected that they will win. Then Hines will not muff a fly, Peters will not make a bad throw, Force and Glenn will bat Spalding for one or more safe hits, Fergy will not make strategy throws to third, there will be another umpire, and the game will be lost or won on its merits.

Chicago Times,
June 4, 1874

In the late 1800s, people were more likely to spend their entire lives in the same town than they are today. That meant intense local loyalties and vociferous intercity rivalries. On June 28, 1875, the Boston Red Stockings and the Philadelphia Athletics were in a tenth-inning tie.

The crowd, however, had pressed closely to the foul line and the ball was stopped and thrown back, so that Fisler only got first. This made a row in that direction, while the crowd poured into the right field. Craver, seeing how Fisler's hit had failed, refused to step to the plate until the crowd was driven back, and an effort was made to do this. There were seven policemen present, but only three appeared to make much effort, and although several of the Athletic nine and two or three of the officers aided, all was in vain. The more respectable portion of the spectators remained in their seats, but a large mob of half-grown boys and roughs poured on the ground. Play, under these circumstances, was impossible, and while the players were wrangling with the mob, and endeavoring to force it back, the rain began and soon poured down.

Philadelphia Times,
June 29, 1875

Whether the situation called for criticism or commendation, reporters were seldom guilty of understatement. The following leads one to wonder whether the Brooklyn Atlantics are a baseball team or victorious crusaders.

Henceforth the 14th of June, 1870 will be regarded as a bright day in the annals of the Atlantic Club of this city, for on that day they achieved the most brilliant victory known in the history of their organization. To win against such a thoroughly trained party of base ball experts as the Red Stockings was in itself a victory to boast of; but to succeed in the face of such adverse circumstances as marked the condition of the club prior to their match with the Cincinnati nine, is a triumph indeed. Take it all in all, it was a model display of the beauties of the game, and a triumph for our Brooklyn Club in which they have a perfect right to glory.

Brooklyn Union,
June 15, 1870

VOL. 1. {THOMPSON & PEARSON,
Publishers.} **NEW YORK, AUGUST 15, 1867.** {HENRY CHADWICK,
Editor.} **No. 11.**

Base Ball.

THE GAME IN NEW YORK.

NEW YORK vs. BROOKLYN.

The Grand Masonic Benefit Match at Brooklyn.

The Finest Picked Nine Match on Record.

TIME OF GAME—ONE HOUR AND FIFTY MINUTES.

Total Score—13 to 7.

Those who remembered the picked nine matches, "New York vs. Brooklyn," played on

Morrisania are the most favored of any, that club making the most efforts to induce the fair sex to grace their games with their presence. A large force of police were present, under the eyes of Superintendent Folk, and the immediate command of Captain Woglom, but their services were not much needed, after the field was cleared for action, excellent order being observed by the assemblage throughout.

New York was represented by nine players respectively from the Mutual, Union, and Active Clubs, and Brooklyn by nine from the Atlantic, Eckford, and Star Clubs. From the Mutual there were the short stop, second baseman, and third baseman, (Devyr, Hatfield, and Pike), each in his home position. From the Union

not only occurred the day before, but also the day after, and as the grounds were, as usual, in excellent order, everything proved to be propitious for a fine contest, the only drawback being half-an-hour's delay, resulting from the absence of two or three of the Brooklyn nine, the New Yorkers putting in a prompt appearance, all being eager for the fray and in prime condition, besides being sanguine of success.

First Innings—The game was appointed for half-past two, but it was 3:05 P. M., before the preliminaries were all arranged and play was called; the thoroughly competent gentleman Mr. John A. Lowell, having been invited to act in the position of umpire. New York was sent

one strike called on him hit another ball so quickly that the umpire, seeing a good ball coming to him and not seeing any movement made to hit it, called "two strikes" simultaneously with Klein's striking the ball, and as the ball was fielded in time to first base to put Klein out, one side called judgment on the out; and the other on the two strikes called. As the error was a palpable one the umpire was fully justified in reversing his decision, and promptly correcting his error by calling out "fair strike." But he held to his decision, and called Klein back to strike. The error might have occasioned a little dispute, but that Klein directly afterwards was put out on a foul fly by Macdiarmid. The occurrence was one that sometimes marks

In 1867 The Ball Players' Chronicle—
*baseball's first weekly—appeared, giving
Chadwick a bully pulpit, which he used
to praise and criticize the game and its
players. His favorite targets were crooked
players and rowdy fans.*

sailors would call 'lobsided;' the position of 'short stop' giving one man more to the left side of the field than the right side. Those handling the ash skillfully have not been slow in discovering the open space between first and second bases and the result has been a decided increase in the average of hits to the right field. To guard this weak point it has been customary for Captains of nines to place their infield in such positions as to cover 'right short' . . . but in doing this the Captains have had to withdraw their men more from the left than is safe, and the result has been an increase in the chances for safe hits to the left and especially over second base, so that what has been gained at right short has been lost by the openings necessarily given in other portions of the infield."

In those days basemen were expected to play close to the bag, both to tag the runner and to defend against fair-foul hits. Chadwick felt that a right shortstop would cut down on the number of fair-foul hits: "with a 'right short' added to the in-field the second baseman is not only enabled to cover his own position and part of the short stop's, but the latter can play up nearer to third, and thereby allow the third baseman to cover the very space which is now open to fair-foul hitting."

Convinced that tighter, lower-scoring games would result from an extra infielder, Chadwick wrote ten-man baseball into his *Clipper* rules for 1874. He expected the change to be approved at the NA convention, but it was not, and Chadwick was rebuffed. He resigned from the rules committee, apparently without bitterness. "We have left to others," he wrote shortly thereafter, "to complete the good work we were engaged in from 1857 to 1874."

From this point on, Chadwick ceased being one of baseball's really big guns. Club officials and owners treated him with respect, his opinions were

taken seriously, but he was never again a truly major player in the baseball world, which was increasingly dominated by the money men represented by his old friend and future employer, Albert Spalding. He was virtually ignored during the National League coup two years later.

Even though Chadwick lost inside influence, his fame and stature continued to grow. He was America's best-known sportswriter, and he had plenty of outlets. As early as 1860 he'd put together the very first guide, *Beadle's Dime Base-Ball Player*, and he'd been responsible for *DeWitt's Guide* from 1869 through 1880. He was associated with the *Brooklyn Eagle* for a large part of his life, although he retired as sports editor in 1894. And he wrote for other papers as well: at one time or another, he wrote for the *Clipper*, the *Times*, the *Herald*, the *World*, the *Sun*, the *Tribune*, the *Mercury*, the *Evening Telegram*, *Sporting Life*, *The Sporting News*, *Outing* and other periodicals around the country. Late in his life, he was best known as the editor of *Spalding's Official Base Ball Guide*. He wrote so many guides and instructional manuals that Harry Wright once joked in a letter that "I do hope he has in print and wish he would publish his 'Instructions & advice to *Presidents.*' "

Chadwick the baseball writer was often an analyst, sometimes a scold, occasionally a cheerleader. He could thunder like a prophet of doom, but he could also sound like an engaging crackpot, as in his adamant opposition to the home run: "A home run is made at the cost to the batsman of a run of 120 yards at his topmost speed, which involves an expenditure of muscular power needing a half hour rest to recuperate from such a violent effort." His complete distrust of the idea of championship games sounds

Far more than just a sportswriter, Chadwick used his medium to advocate adjustments in the way the game was played. He railed against the imbalance of the infield (as shown in the sheet music above), calling for a second shortstop to play between first and second. With the New York Clipper *(above, right), Chadwick wrote about other sports as well as baseball, including yachting and billiards.*

By 1870 even kids had caught on to the innocent fun of baseball, and school teams began to arise. In this photograph, the Washington School Nine takes on a school from New Milford at a field in Danbury, Connecticut.

In baseball's early days, many clubs held their meetings in saloons, and most fans tipped back a few before, during and after games. Fighting all this was Chadwick, baseball's voice for temperance. His constant diatribes against the ills of alcohol had at best a marginal effect on the link between baseball and beer.

Chadwick worked to change the rule that a ball caught on one bounce was an out, and "Catch It on the Fly" was one of his favorite theme songs. "Nothing disappoints the spectator, or dissatisfies the batsmen so much, as to see a fine hit to the long field caught on the bound in this simple, childish manner," he wrote.

similarly strange to modern baseball fans: "We do not think this championship business has any healthy effect on the game." But there are many more moments in Chadwick's writings where he appears to be caught up in the sheer beauty of the game. Describing an 1867 game between the National Club of Washington and the Excelsiors of Chicago, Chadwick writes that Excelsior batter Blakeslee "then sent a hot one to Fox, who grasped the ball when Blakeslee was within a few yards of the base, and sending it to Fletcher almost like an arrow from a bow, and the ball being held in splendid style, the astonished Connecticut gent found himself cut off in his prime."

Chadwick also wrote uncompromisingly against gambling and the crookedness it brought to baseball. Later, he turned his fire on drunkenness in the ranks of players. Owners and club officials didn't always appreciate reading about the underside of their sport in Chadwick's columns. He infuriated Chicago's William Hulbert—founder of the National League—so thoroughly that Boston's Harry Wright felt compelled to defend Chadwick: "You Western folks do pitch into him unmercifully. Now what has he done to deserve it all? Does he not, and has he not always supported honest & honorable playing & players?"

Yet even Wright felt that baseball needed some protection from Chadwick's assaults: "It would have been better at times—looking at it from a distance—had he said less about 'queer games' and 'suspicious play,' & 'crooked players,' for it only served to disgust the public and cause them to regard *all* games with suspicion, without in the least abating the evils that he intended it should. I have been provoked time & again when reading his no-

tices of certain games, and I can imagine how they would affect others who were at all lukewarm in their support of the game."

Chadwick wasn't always pronouncing on grand questions. As a working reporter, he shared less elevated concerns with every sportswriter who ever covered an event. In the early 1870s he urged William Cammeyer, owner of the Union Grounds, to improve "the old tumble-down inconvenient reporters' stand. It ought to be removed about ten or fifteen yards further back and raised, or boarded up behind, to prevent the members of the press from being annoyed by outsiders gazing over their shoulders to see how the game stands."

As much as anything, though, Chadwick, in his columns and notices, was a teacher. During most of his career, the country was coming to love baseball, but didn't yet fully understand it. Today, many of his columns sound jarringly pedantic, but they also illuminate the gradual development of the game. In an 1873 survey of outfielders, for example, he wrote, "It has become the duty of outfielders to 'back up' more than was formerly deemed necessary, it now being regarded as very loose fielding for any outfielder to fail to be active in backing up the moment any ball goes outside the infield."

Chadwick lectured management as well as fans. And some of his ideas were ahead of his time. In 1872 he wrote on the subject of relievers: "The change pitcher should be made more frequently available than he is. For instance, it does not follow that the regular man should not be changed until he is badly 'punished' for by that time the opposing nine have gained a confidence in batting which is an element of success in itself and one that even a change of pitchers will not always remove. The time to change is when the opposing

Another thing Chadwick opposed was the home run. He felt it was an inefficient use of energy and claimed that home run hitters "generally [had] the poorest average of bases on hits," a statistic he called "the only true criterion of a batsman's skill."

Before the advent of the press box, the official scorer was stationed at his own table, as in the far right of this engraving of an 1866 game. Chadwick's influence on the game may have been greatest in the area of how games are scored, and his invention of the box score flung open the door of examination into the numbers behind the game.

nine are beginning to be familiar with the regular pitcher's tactics; then it is that the change pitcher should be brought in if only for an innings or two."

As Father grew older, he got crankier. Although he appreciated their skill, he had little use for the generation of professional ballplayers who took the field in the 1880s and 1890s, constantly berating them for drunkenness, greed, unsportsmanlike behavior and general all-around degeneracy. "The League season of 1894," he wrote in the *Spalding Guide*, "was characterized by 'hoodlumism.' " This word, as he described it, "is a technical term applicable to the use of *blackguard language; low cunning tricks,* unworthy of manly players; *brutal assaults* on umpire and players; that nuisance of our ball fields, 'kicking,' and the dishonorable methods comprised in the term *dirty ball playing."*

During the 1880s, club owners imposed the reserve rule and strict salary limits in a successful attempt to keep payrolls down and players from moving on. Frustrated and angry, most of the game's best players joined to create their own circuit—the Players' League—in 1890. Chadwick had no sympathy for them. He was, as a colleague said at the time, "an out and out, died-in-the-wool League man."

This certainly had something to do with his relationship with his employer, Albert Spalding, who was the National League's chief strategist in the war against the players. But it was also a true reflection of Chadwick's attitude toward the modern ballplayer. He made no bones about his feelings in his writings—especially "Chadwick's Chat," his famous column in *Sporting Life.* "Gratitude for favors shown them," he wrote, "is something unknown in the vocabulary of a professional ball player."

After the turn of the century, Chadwick hardly slowed down, although his health had begun to plague him by the late 1890s. His "Chat" remained a popular feature to baseball fans around the country, and he still put out the annual *Spalding Guide*. His work habits were exemplary. He got up at five, took his customary "cold plunge," ate a light breakfast and got to work "before the ordinary city man is stirring." Never a stick-in-the-mud, he had for years been using the newfangled typewriter. In his leisure time, he tickled other keys, playing the piano for friends.

Henry Chadwick met his final deadline on April 20, 1908, after catching pneumonia at Brooklyn's opening day game against the New York Giants. He was 83 years old, and he'd chronicled everything in baseball from the Knickerbockers to Ty Cobb, from genteel, amateur exercise to the slashing, aggressive inside game of John McGraw. Father had seen it all. ◗◖

Since Chadwick (shown here shortly before his death in 1908) was baseball's first great scribe, it was only fitting that he be the first of his profession to be inducted into the Hall of Fame, as he was in 1938. As far as baseball was concerned, he not only took care of who, what, when and where, but also how (below).

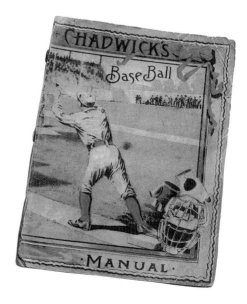

The Men in Black

U mpires weren't always the scapegoats that they are today. The earliest umpires had it easy; they lounged off to the side of the field, ruling on controversial plays only, not bothering to call balls or strikes. They were often chosen from among club members—Alexander Cartwright frequently called the Knickerbockers' matches—or from among spectators.

When interclub matches became more frequent, teams provided an umpire apiece, and a third, neutral referee was chosen to mediate—all in an effort to keep games fair.

But fairness wasn't always the rule. Umpires weren't always knowledgeable about the game, and they weren't always taken seriously. In fact, until 1882, umpires could ask *spectators* for advice when making a call.

In 1857 the Liberty Club of New Jersey was challenged by a pickup team called, appropriately, the Foundlings. For their umpire, the Foundlings selected a man who, according to the *New York Clipper,* "was almost entirely ignorant of the game." The Liberty Club provided both an umpire and a referee, neither of whom made an effort to disguise his bias, calling the Foundlings "out" and the Liberty players "safe" on all but the most obvious plays. "At the last innings," wrote the *Clipper,* "the Foundlings having the bat, and two men out, it being at the time almost dark, this model of a referee got engaged in a very interesting conversation with an out-sider, and while so engaged, a ball was knocked foul; some said it was caught, others said it was not; the umpire could not decide, and the referee was called upon for his decision. He instantly said it was out, but in the same breath said *he did not see the ball caught.*" As for the score of the game at the end of nine, the Foundlings'

man had it a 32–32 tie; the Libertys' umpire had his club ahead, 32–31, leaving it to the referee to decide. "He, with his usual justice," went the *Clipper* account, "said the Liberty had made 32 and the Foundlings 29 runs. This caused a general laugh among all parties." The referee then changed his scorecard so that it agreed with the Liberty umpire's, and the Liberty Club took the game, 32–31. Considering the referee's behavior, the *Clipper* reporter—not to mention the spectators and the players—showed remarkable restraint. Imagine what an Earl Weaver or a Billy Martin would have done.

The tradition of abusing umpires seems to have started later, perhaps with the founding of the NL in 1876, when club owners decided that umpires would no longer be good-natured volunteers but paid professionals. Soon afterwards, "the kicking problem" —the controversy over the right of players and managers to argue an umpire's call—became a hot topic. Henry Chadwick, always the conservative, claimed that the rules strictly forbade it and that arguing allowed a player to "indulge his bad temper." Albert Spalding countered, saying that players and managers were merely exercising their democratic rights by rebelling against the tyranny of the umpire.

But arguing was just the beginning. And today's practice of kicking dirt on the umpire's shoes seems mild compared with what happened on two occasions—in Alabama in 1889 and in Indiana in 1891—when umpires were struck with bats and killed. Ironically, the first to introduce the bat into player-umpire disputes was an umpire. In the early 1870s umpire Bob Ferguson whacked a New York Mutuals catcher who had called him a liar, proving that umpires have not always been the victims.

Mother, may I slug the umpire,
May I slug him right away,
So he cannot be here, mother,
When the clubs begin to play?
Let me clasp his throat, dear mother,
In a dear, delightful grip,
With one hand, and with the other
Bat him several in the lip.

Chicago Tribune, *August 15, 1886*

Umpiring has changed in many respects since
the early days of baseball, one of the most
obvious being that umpires no longer bring
their own furniture to the field. But Henry
Chadwick's description of the job's difficulties
holds true today. The "position of an Umpire is
an honorable one," he wrote, "but its duties
are anything but agreeable, as it is next to
impossible to give entire satisfaction to all
parties concerned in a match."

The Pitcher

Diamond Dust

Trial and error were the hallmarks of America's popular young sport. Baseball's rules, its tactics and its structure were evolving from the moment the Knickerbockers drew up their few simple rules in the 1840s. Though some of the early changes led to dead ends and were eventually scrapped, many became permanent because they improved the game. At its convention in 1860, the old amateur National Association decided that teams should play extra innings to decide games tied at the end of nine. In 1864 the NA decreed that baserunners circling the bases actually had to *touch* them, not just come close. That same year the NA finally accepted the Knickerbockers' proposal that a ball had to be caught on the fly to become an out. Today such rules seem natural, but each was the result of some problem that players and officials resolved to fix.

Players often took matters into their own hands, sometimes testing the rules, sometimes breaking them. In 1865 Eddie Cuthbert of the Philadelphia Keystones simply "took" second base at the Capitoline Grounds in Brooklyn without advancing on a hit, and fans and players alike laughed at him. But when officials realized that there was no rule against the tactic, Cuthbert was allowed to remain at second and the stolen base was born.

But there *was* a rule against pitchers throwing the ball to the plate with bent elbow and snapped wrist. From the start, a pitch was supposed to be a simple, straight-armed, underhand toss. Officials fought an unsuccessful

In 1872 the NA finally allowed what some pitchers had been using illegally for years—a wrist snap during delivery. The rule brought pitchers better fastballs and curves, and run production fell from 9.8 per game in 1871 to 6.3 in 1875.

"I FEEL IT WHEN I SORROW MOST."

In baseball's early days, control problems weren't really problems at all, since pitchers could throw anywhere from five to nine balls before a batter took his base. Still, marginal players known as "muffins" (as in this drawing from Base Ball as Viewed by a Muffin) *were lampooned for their lack of control.*

four-decade battle against pitchers who had the audacity to try to foil the batter instead of simply delivering the ball. Almost from the beginning, pitchers tried to get around the restriction. By 1860 one of them had succeeded spectacularly. Jim Creighton ignored the rule, using what Henry Chadwick called an "underhand throw," and got the ball over the plate with pace. He somehow got away with it and became a great fastballer and the game's first dominant pitcher.

Suddenly everybody wanted to steam the ball in there. Many could do that, but few had Creighton's control. Baseball was suddenly full of pitchers who couldn't get the ball over the plate because they were trying so hard to pitch fast. Of course, some of them didn't always *want* to get the ball over the plate. For the 1864 season, the NA directed that the pitcher "must deliver the ball as near as possible over the center of the home base, and for the striker." Chadwick wrote that this last phrase was included "to do away with the unfair style of pitching that was in vogue during 1861, '62 and '63 . . . by trying to intimidate the batsmen by pitching the ball *at* them instead of *for* them as the rules require." That's a roundabout way of saying that the brush-back pitch made its appearance early.

Lack of control in those days wasn't the problem it later became: until the mid-1860s, there was no such thing as a called ball, and called strikes had been around only a few years. When rulemakers finally realized that they had to do something to keep the game moving, they eased into it gently. If a pitcher threw two successive bad pitches, the umpire had to warn him to deliver the "ball to the bat." Only then could the umpire start calling balls. The batter took his base after "ball three"—which was really at least "ball five."

If the batter consistently failed to swing at pitches that were "within the legitimate reach of the bat," he got a similar warning. Then it was "strike one," "strike two," "strike three"—but really at least "strike four" before he was out. Called strikes were relatively rare: George Wright claimed years later that "it was an unwritten law that the hitter should do his utmost to connect with the ball."

As pitchers' speed increased, so did catchers' insurance rates. But in 1875 Harvard captain Fred Thayer, who wanted his catcher to stand closer to the plate, designed baseball's first catcher's mask.

Baseball history books show that in 1879 a walk required nine balls. Actually, it wasn't quite that simple: the umpire was directed to call a ball after every third "wide." Three called balls—or a total of nine wides—gave the batter his base. At this time, the pitcher worked from within a chalked box six feet square, the front edge of which was 45 feet from the plate. There was no mound; if anything, pitchers scuffed a depression in the ground that got deeper as the game went on. A pitcher could take several steps forward with his delivery, but he was not allowed to step over that front line. The pitched ball flew over a grassless "alley" between the pitcher's and batter's boxes.

Despite rules designed to restrict the effect that pitchers could have on the game, wily hurlers never stopped expanding the possibilities of their craft. By the late 1860s they introduced what Cap Anson called "the greatest change ever made in the National Game": the curveball. The first well-known curveballer was twirler Candy Cummings, who later claimed that he developed his breaking ball in 1867, first using it effectively when pitching for the Brooklyn Excelsiors against Harvard College. To batters, the pitch was an unpleasant revelation; to other pitchers, it was an inspiration. By 1869 a few, like the Cincinnati Red Stockings' Asa Brainard, were throwing curves them-

Kansas City's Dan Quisenberry—and other submarine-style pitchers—are the closest thing modern fans will see to 19th-century pitching. Quisenberry has the advantage of throwing from a mound, but old-time hurlers were 15 feet closer to home plate.

selves. Cummings had a short career in which he won almost two-thirds of his games. But his downfall turned out to be problems with management; in the six years that he pitched as a professional, he moved to a new team every year but one.

Cummings used a sort of submarine delivery with a twist of the wrist. Contemporaries called his motion "a horizontal whip." Although he and most other pitchers had thrown this way for several years, it wasn't made legal until 1872. After that, a pitcher was allowed to snap or jerk the ball as long as his hand remained below his waist during the delivery. Facing a pitcher in the 1870s was a lot like facing Dan Quisenberry from 15 yards away.

Many baseball people worried that allowing pitchers to get around the rules would enable them to overwhelm batters with speed. Chadwick spoke for the majority, though, when he argued otherwise. He claimed that the *catcher* would be a limiting factor on pitching speed. As usual, he was right: a bare-handed man simply cannot reliably catch a ball thrown as hard as possible from 45 feet away. But in the 1880s mitts appeared. And although they were little more than work gloves at first, catchers began modifying them so that they could handle harder and harder pitches. To protect the batters, in 1881 rulemakers moved the pitching box back to 50 feet. Then, in 1893, after the advent of large, well-padded catchers' mitts, the rules set the rubber—and by this time it was on a mound—at 60 feet 6 inches from the plate.

Trying to keep things balanced after deciding to allow pitchers to throw with a wrist snap, the National Association declared in 1870 that batters could call for high or low pitches. Depending on the hitter's preference, the pitcher had to deliver the ball either between the shoulders and the waist or between the waist and a point a foot from the ground. This "high/low pitch" rule was

A FAIR DELIVERY.

It will be seen by the above illustration what the rule means by the words, "with the arm swinging nearly perpendicular at the side of the body." This is the delivery of a pitch, a toss, a jerk, or an underhand throw, the ball in each case passing below the line of the hip as the hand holding it is swung forward in delivery.

AN ILLEGAL DELIVERY.

The rule governing the delivery of the ball requires that the ball shall be swung forward *below* the line of the hip. It will be seen that the pitcher in the above cut is delivering the ball on the line of the hip, instead of below that line, as the rule requires.

The line between fair and foul pitching was especially blurry from 1872 to 1883, when pitchers were allowed to snap their wrists but had to release the ball below the waist. The DeWitt Guide *(above) illustrated the do's and don'ts.*

retained by the National League and lasted for 18 seasons through 1887. And while the idea of the batter telling the pitcher where to throw seems odd, it was not as quaint as it sounds. Neither zone is any smaller than the one called by most major league umpires today.

By the time throwing became legal in 1872, there was only one "true pitcher" left in baseball—one who delivered the ball underhand with a straight arm. He was Alphonse Martin—"Old Slow Ball Phonnie"—who labored for the Troy Haymakers and, at the end of his career, the New York Mutuals. Martin was known for tossing a very slow backspinning pitch that seemed to die at the plate. His best years were behind him by the time the professional National Association was formed, and the new generation of hitters quickly made his style of pitching obsolete. "Old Slow Ball" was 3–12 in his two years with the NA.

For the 1873 season, Cummings swapped teams with the other great breaking-ball pitcher of the time, Bobby Mathews: Cummings moved to the Lord Baltimores, and Mathews to the Mutuals. *The Baseball Encyclopedia* shows Mathews at 5' 5½", 140 pounds, but at least one contemporary dressed him out at a tiny 5' ½", 110 pounds. His specialty was a "weird twister," something new to baseball. "Mathews was able to get a wonderful drop on the ball, and he controlled with remarkable skill," recalled Hank O'Day, who pitched for several American Association and NL teams in the 1880s and later became a well-known National League umpire. "Mathews used to cover the palm of his left hand with saliva and then rub the ball in it, twisting the leather around until there was a white spot on it as big as a silver quarter. The pitchers didn't wear gloves on their left hands in those

5' 11" 175 lbs. b 1849
BR TR d 10/10/1883

JIM DEVLIN

In 1877 Louisville Gray pitcher Jim Devlin found his career cut short by scandal. He was the game's dominant pitcher that season, but by the next year he was its most pathetic figure.

Originally an infielder, Devlin was in his third professional year in 1875 when he began to pitch, going 6–16 for the Chicago White Stockings. Henry Chadwick wrote that Devlin needed "practice in getting command of the ball."

When the 1876 season came around, Devlin moved to the Louisville Grays, where he not only took command of the ball but enslaved it. Through that season and the next, Devlin pitched virtually all of his team's games, and led the league both years in games, complete games and innings pitched.

But in late 1877 Devlin confessed to throwing games in what became the famous Louisville scandal and was barred from professional ball for life. Uneducated and unprepared for life without baseball, Devlin begged for reinstatement. "I have not got a Stich of Clothing or has my wife and child," he wrote to Harry Wright, "do something for me I am honest Harry you need not Be afraid." Wright refused.

Devlin then appealed to his friend, NL President William Hulbert. In a heart-rending scene that had both men in tears, Hulbert pressed $50 into Devlin's palm but would not rescind the life suspension. Devlin died destitute five years later.

Continued on page 142

Deacon White

Gambling, drinking and smoking seemed as natural to most ballplayers of the 1870s as hitting a baseball. Not so with abstemious James White, the best bare-handed catcher of his era, who was nicknamed "Deacon" for his sober manner and churchgoing ways.

Yet White was a man who challenged the rules, innovated on the field and was a great slugger to boot. In a professional career that spanned 20 years, he changed the role of the catcher, hit over .300 in 12 seasons and led the NL in 1877 with a .387 average. And off the field, he was an advocate of players' rights.

Baseball historian David Voigt names White as the first catcher to stand close behind home plate. In the days of bare-handed play, the catcher stood well back from the batter and caught the ball on the bounce. White's development of a rudimentary catcher's glove and mask in the late 1870s enabled him to move up right behind the plate, and he reputedly introduced the idea that the catcher should provide the pitcher a target.

White first gained national recognition in 1873 with the Boston Red Stockings of the National Association, where he and pitcher Al Spalding were the most feared battery in the league. One of their practices was the "quick pitch," with White rapidly returning a pitched ball to Spalding, who immediately fired it back to the plate, much to the surprise of the batter.

In his first year at Boston, White posted a .382 average. Teammates Ross Barnes, Cal McVey, Spalding and White became known as "the Big Four" and led Boston to three successive pennants, 1873 through 1875. Just before the end of the 1875 season, a *Chicago Tribune* sportswriter leaked the news

that the Big Four had signed with Chicago for the next year. The news sent Boston into shock, and the four players were hissed and booed for the rest of the season, even though the Red Stockings finished first with a 71–8 record. Signing early with another team was a common practice, but the act itself was illegal by NA rules. Still, no reserve clause existed then, and contracts were good for only one year.

In 1876, the first year of the NL, Chicago compiled a 52–14 record and took the pennant, White led the league in RBI with 60 and Boston finished fourth. The next year, White returned to Boston, and in addition to leading the league in batting average, he led in hits with 103, triples with 11, RBI with 49 and slugging average with .545. His fielding—he played several games at first base and in the outfield—was solid, and his performance helped propel Boston to its first NL pennant.

In 1888, toward the end of his long career, while White was with Detroit, he and teammate Jack Rowe were sold to Pittsburgh for $7,000. The move angered the pair because they received only a fraction of the money. By then, White and Rowe were owners of an International League franchise in Buffalo. They refused to go to Pittsburgh, saying they would play with Buffalo. The two brought the reserve clause—and the larger question of player treatment—into the public eye. Because of problems with their Buffalo team, White and Rowe finally agreed to play for Pittsburgh, but for the handsome sum of $1,250 each and a salary of $500 a month.

White told a reporter, "We are satisfied with the money, but we ain't worth it. Rowe's arm is gone. I'm over 40 and my fielding ain't so good, though I can still hit some. But I will say this. No man is going to sell my carcass unless I get half."

A century of catchers owe a debt to Deacon White, who, with Buffalo teammate Jim O'Rourke, designed baseball's first chest protector in 1884. White's innovative approach to protective equipment helped him last as a player from 1868 to 1891.

DEACON WHITE

Third Base, Catcher
Cleveland Forest Citys 1868–1870
National Association
Cleveland Forest Citys 1871–1872
Boston Red Stockings 1873–1875
National League
Chicago White Stockings 1876
Boston Red Stockings 1877
Cincinnati Red Stockings 1878–1880
Buffalo Bisons 1881–1885
Detroit Wolverines 1886–1888
Pittsburgh Pirates 1889
Players League
Buffalo Bisons 1890

GAMES	**1,558**
AT-BATS	**6,651**
BATTING AVERAGE	
Career	**.312**
Season High	**.387**
HITS	
Career	**2,075**
Season High	**157**
BATTING TITLE	**1877**
RUNS	
Career	**1,136**
Season High	**82**
DOUBLES (NL, PL only)	
Career	**217**
Season High	**24**
TRIPLES (NL, PL only)	
Career	**73**
Season High	**11**
HOME RUNS (NL, PL only)	
Career	**18**
Season High	**5**
RUNS BATTED IN (NL, PL only)	
Career	**602**
Season High	**76**

Combined NA, NL and PL stats unless otherwise noted

JACK CHAPMAN
Outfield

5' 11" 170 lbs.
TR

b 5/8/1843
d 6/10/1916

In the 1860s the gentlemanly school of baseball was giving way to a new breed—ballplayers who played only to win. Many of the older players were pushed into retirement by the more demanding style, but one player who was at home in both camps was out-fielder Jack Chapman. Chapman played most of his career in his hometown of Brooklyn, debuting with the Putnams in 1860 and playing 9 of his 15 seasons for the Atlantics.

Despite his normally restrained de-meanor, there was nothing reserved about the way Chapman played once the game started. In an era when few fielders caught balls on the fly, the *New York Clipper* said, "We have seen him run at full speed, either toward the diamond or into deep left field and make the most surprising one-handed catches as we have seen no other fielder do."

Chapman, always the Victorian gentleman, was respected by his col-leagues and canonized in the press. He remained above the fray when team rivalries overheated, and though sur-rounded by ballplayers who sold games to gamblers, he was never regarded with even a hint of suspicion.

In 1877 Chapman's rapidly expand-ing girth forced him into a managerial role, which he performed on and off until 1892. Perhaps he was too much the gentleman for the rough and rowdy baseball of the changing times; he had only two winning seasons out of ten as a manager and retired with a 306–428 lifetime record.

days, and if a ball was fouled into the stands it was brought back. Every time Mathews pitched, therefore, we noticed the white spot on the ball, which was due to saliva."

In 1914, when O'Day was writing, the spitball was well known, but in the 1880s few had ever seen a spitter. Even more impressive, O'Day re-called that "Mathews, like other noted pitchers had an out-curve, inshoot or fast ball, a drop and a raise ball. In fact, he was able to deliver everything now used by modern pitchers." Another writer recalled that Mathews never dis-cussed his technique: "Mathews was the Sphinx of baseball. He only smiled when asked about his methods." Gaylord Perry would understand.

Naturally, pitchers weren't satisfied with the 1872 requirement that they throw from below the waist; many actually delivered from just below the shoulder. By the late 1870s, Tommy Bond was winning big for Boston, and one observer wrote that Bond would be effective for years to come "unless his style is ruled out as unfair." Tommy threw his "parabolic curve" sidearm.

In 1878 Bond took part in one of the first demonstrations to prove that curveballs really curve. One day in Cincinnati, members of the Red Stockings set up two parallel ten-foot fences some 20 yards apart, with a post between them. Bond stood to the left of one fence and threw ball after ball that went to the right of the post but finished to the left of the second fence. When skeptics claimed that the wind was moving the ball, Cincinnati's Bobby Mitchell, a left-hander, repeated the exhibition in reverse. From the right of the first fence, his tosses passed to the left of the post, then back to the right of the second fence. Proof that a curveball actually curves was telegraphed all over

the country, but it failed to put the controversy to rest, and similar demonstrations were held well into the 20th century.

The curve wasn't just a mystery to the general public and to the men trying to hit it. Catchers had a lot of trouble with the pitch, too. They typically stood well back from the batter and took the ball on the hop. A pitch like Cummings' "difficult bias delivery" spun so hard when it hit the ground that it always took an "eccentric rebound."As a result, catchers—always in danger of taking more than their fair share of lumps—were getting battered. Long after the founding of the National League in 1876, receivers played with virtually no protective equipment. One 1905 volume described the old-time catcher's job this way: "Working behind the bat without mask, glove, or chest protector, he had to be as graceful and quick as a cat, even to live."

Nat Hicks, who caught both Cummings and Mathews for the Mutuals, was a good representative of this tough breed of backstops. During the 1873 season, he had to leave a game when he was hit by a foul tip. He returned the next day only to take another hard foul smack in the mouth. This time he took a drink, wiped off the blood and went back to work. *The New York Times* wrote that he was hit a total of four times during the game: "on the mouth, chest and twice with the bat. He played with his right eye almost knocked out of his head, his nose and the whole right side of his face swollen three times normal size."

The following year, catcher Hicks was bowled over by Dave Eggler of the Philadelphias, who "shut him up like a jack knife. Hicks seemed badly injured and rolled on the grass, tried to faint, loosened his belt, took a big swig of Cammeyer's whiskey and proceeded with the game." A tough cookie, Mr. Hicks.

In baseball's early days the catcher stood closer to the batter than did the pitcher, but not by that much. Primitive gloves, masks and chest protectors brought backstops a little closer, but it wasn't until the late 1870s that most catchers were brave enough to stand directly behind the plate.

"A HIT, A VERY PALPABLE HIT."

There was little that could protect a catcher in the 1870s from a bat to the face, but in the latter part of the decade Boston star shortstop George Wright introduced a protective rubber mouthpiece for catchers that was guaranteed not to have "any disagreeable taste."

By the mid-1870s, some catchers were beginning to use rubber mouthpieces to keep from getting smashed teeth, but masks were still a few years away, and chest protectors and shin guards were decades in the future. Yet catchers weren't the only players faced with injury. First basemen had to take hot throws from infielders with their bare hands, too. Charlie Gould of the Red Stockings won a measure of fame by fielding "regular finger-breakers" from the rifle-armed George Wright.

But it wasn't just hard throws that caused problems. The ball used in the NA during the 1870s was hard and relatively lively, and grounders were always a potential hazard to bare-handed infielders. Bob Ferguson—an outstanding third baseman for the Mutuals and the Atlantics and president of the NA several times—gloried in the nickname "Death to Flying Things," a tribute to his ability to handle fly balls. Later in life he commented on how he and his colleagues had managed to handle grounders without a glove: "In those days the balls came to you red hot, and it was a frequent occurrence to see a player knocked off his feet by them. Some players will shin the ball, that is, they will stop it with their shins with the intention of picking it up quickly, but in doing this the ball is apt to bound away from them. Again, some players will 'crowd' a ball, by dropping on it with their hands and knees, but unless they are very quick they are not able to recover themselves in time. Then I have seen players 'draw,' the ball, as it is called, by standing in front of it with legs close together and let the ball run up to their hands. This is the worst of the lot, for if the ground is in any way rough the ball is sure to bound away to one side. The perfect plan is the one which I always used, and that is to scoop the ball as it comes to you. This I do by holding the hands close together and give the arms full play. As the ball comes up let the hands go back between the legs

Bare-handed fielding disappeared from baseball in the 1890s, but you can still glimpse this lost art on cricket pitches all over the world.

slightly, and when the ball is about a foot from you, suddenly bring the hands forward and run the fingers under the ball. It is easy and sure."

A number of Ferguson's peers had fine reputations as fielders and probably handled hard-hit ground balls as well as they can be handled without a glove. George Wright must have been a veritable Victorian Ozzie Smith: "His hands, his arms, his whole body yielded to the impact; his 'set' for his throw was only a continuation of the movement by which he caught the ball." But observers who saw both old-time bare-handed baseball and the gloved game of the early 20th century insist that infield play in the older game was slower. One writer put it this way: "To take a fast throw or grounder without gloves and especially if the ball is elastic and heavy, one must give to it, must 'ease up on it.' And that delays the throw."

There was great raw athletic talent around during the 1860s and 1870s. In a tournament in Brooklyn featuring the Red Stockings, the Athletics and the Mutuals, New York's John Hatfield won the throwing competition and $25 by beating Andy Leonard, George Wright, Bill Boyd and Adrian Anson with a throw of 400 feet 7½ inches. Compare that with a similar contest almost 50 years later that included Babe Ruth, Ty Cobb, Shoeless Joe Jackson and Tris Speaker. Jackson won with a heave of 397 feet.

Players were using their heads as well as their hands. Red Stocking second baseman Ross Barnes, perhaps baseball's greatest player during the professional NA era, confused baserunners with phantom tags. Modern infielders, who use this tactic constantly, should be grateful for the precedent.

Like George Wright, shortstop Dickey Pearce of the Atlantics liked to double runners off "on a prettily dropped fly ball." With men on first and sec-

Continued on page 148

Gearing Up

In baseball's turbulent infancy, uniforms began to serve as a sort of caste system; the quality and uniformity of a team's dress said a great deal about the quality and seriousness of its play. Teams that showed up in less than full dress were chided by the press. "Get new uniforms, gentlemen, if you can afford it, and wear them whenever you play ball, if you want to look like ball-players," wrote a reporter for *Wilkes' Spirit of the Times* in 1864.

By the 1870s things got a little flashier, and in 1876 Al Spalding went so far as to provide a different colored hat for each position. The effect, according to the *Chicago Tribune,* made the team look like a "Dutch bed of tulips."

Red, white and blue provided the color spectrum for most baseball teams, but players had to provide their own green. Players in the National League in 1877 not only had to pay $30 a year for uniforms, they had to shell out for laundry too.

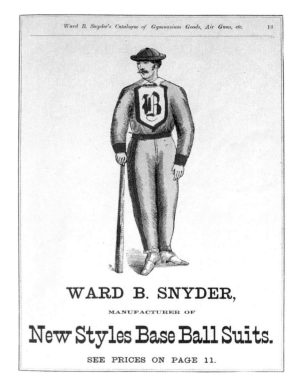

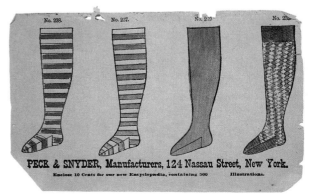

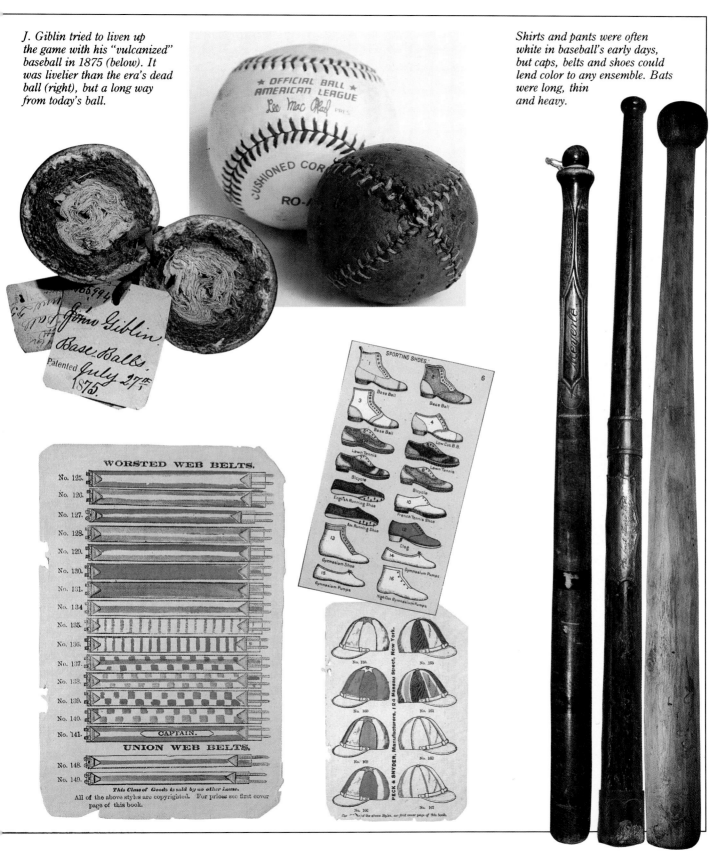

J. Giblin tried to liven up the game with his "vulcanized" baseball in 1875 (below). It was livelier than the era's dead ball (right), but a long way from today's ball.

Shirts and pants were often white in baseball's early days, but caps, belts and shoes could lend color to any ensemble. Bats were long, thin and heavy.

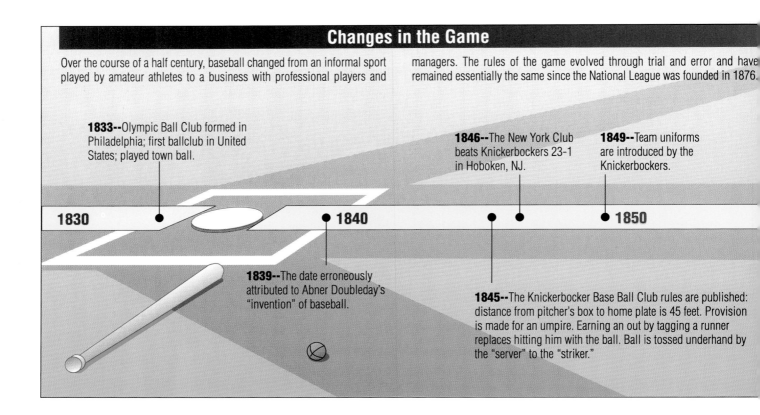

Changes in the Game

Over the course of a half century, baseball changed from an informal sport played by amateur athletes to a business with professional players and managers. The rules of the game evolved through trial and error and have remained essentially the same since the National League was founded in 1876.

1833--Olympic Ball Club formed in Philadelphia; first ballclub in United States; played town ball.

1846--The New York Club beats Knickerbockers 23-1 in Hoboken, NJ.

1849--Team uniforms are introduced by the Knickerbockers.

1830

1840

1850

1839--The date erroneously attributed to Abner Doubleday's "invention" of baseball.

1845--The Knickerbocker Base Ball Club rules are published: distance from pitcher's box to home plate is 45 feet. Provision is made for an umpire. Earning an out by tagging a runner replaces hitting him with the ball. Ball is tossed underhand by the "server" to the "striker."

ond, and a pop fly to the infield, the infielder purposely dropped the ball and began a third-to-second twin killing, victimizing baserunners who had been holding their bases. Henry Chadwick actually recommended that the fielder shouldn't catch and drop the ball, lest the umpire call the batter out; he should hold his palms flat and let the ball bounce off them. In 1895 the infield fly rule spoiled everything.

Things were happening on the offensive side, too. In an 1872 game against the Mutuals, the Red Stockings' Barnes ran for pitcher Spalding. What's strange about that? Well, Spalding went up to the plate and swung the bat—Barnes just *ran* for him. The Red Stockings were certainly "big league," but that particular play was eventually relegated to the playground.

In most other ways, except for uniforms and equipment, baseball of the 1870s was quite similar to the game we see today. A lively ball was used in the NA, a ball much livelier than the one adopted by the National League, and nearly as energetic as the one that Babe Ruth used a half century later. Batters responded quickly. As one observer later said, "The batter slugged and slugged and slugged. He held his bat tightly by the extreme end, planted himself squarely on his two feet, and swung with all his might."

But there was strategy at the plate, too. Until 1877 the fair-foul hit was playable and was very hard for fielders to chase down. And players often got extra bases when the ball took strange hops or bounded well away from the field. In 1874 a Red Stockings player somehow spun a ball into fair territory that promptly bounced back over the catcher's head and out the grandstand gate. Home run.

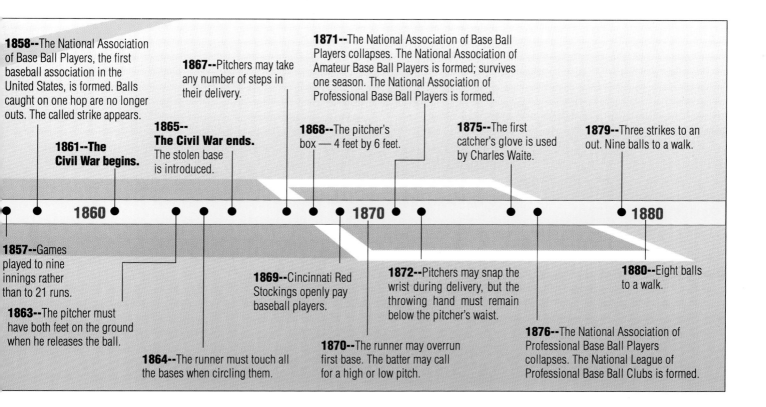

1858--The National Association of Base Ball Players, the first baseball association in the United States, is formed. Balls caught on one hop are no longer outs. The called strike appears.

1867--Pitchers may take any number of steps in their delivery.

1871--The National Association of Base Ball Players collapses. The National Association of Amateur Base Ball Players is formed; survives one season. The National Association of Professional Base Ball Players is formed.

1861--The Civil War begins.

1865-- The Civil War ends. The stolen base is introduced.

1868--The pitcher's box — 4 feet by 6 feet.

1875--The first catcher's glove is used by Charles Waite.

1879--Three strikes to an out. Nine balls to a walk.

1860   1870   1880

1857--Games played to nine innings rather than to 21 runs.

1863--The pitcher must have both feet on the ground when he releases the ball.

1869--Cincinnati Red Stockings openly pay baseball players.

1872--Pitchers may snap the wrist during delivery, but the throwing hand must remain below the pitcher's waist.

1880--Eight balls to a walk.

1864--The runner must touch all the bases when circling them.

1870--The runner may overrun first base. The batter may call for a high or low pitch.

1876--The National Association of Professional Base Ball Players collapses. The National League of Professional Base Ball Clubs is formed.

Rulemakers tried for years to do something about the fair-foul hit without actually banning it. Their most frequent strategy was to move home plate. Home base had begun as a circular disk—a "plate" of metal or wood or stone. By the early 1860s, iron was specified, and the plate itself was eight-sided rather than circular. It was set inside the angle of the first- and third-base lines, much as the modern plate is. By the late 1860s, home plate had become diamond-shaped and had been moved back so that its center sat over the intersection of the two baselines—part of it was in foul territory. By 1875 the plate lay entirely in foul ground, its forward tip just touching the point where the baselines met. As the plate was moved back, batters had to move back with it. The farther back the batters moved, the harder it was for them to hit fair territory with a grounder headed foul. The modern five-sided plate, located entirely within fair territory, was not standard until 1900.

The men who had to keep up to date on the game's constant changes were the umpires. One per game was considered plenty, and in the earliest days he often sat off to the side in a chair like a tennis official. Later he stood—sometimes with a low bench to prop one foot on. Early NA regulations required that the umps "must keep a record of the game in a book prepared for the purpose." His dual role as arbiter and scorekeeper wasn't as onerous as it sounds, because at first umpires didn't have a call to make on every play—they only ruled on the controversial ones.

Soon enough, though, the umpire's job got tougher. But even in the professional NA, there was no regular crew of umps. Arranging for one to handle a game was an almost courtly process. The visiting team submitted a list of five names to the home club. All were supposed to "be known as com-

THE RED DEAD BALL!!!

The Undersigned call the attention of the Base Ball fraternity and of Dealers in Base Ball Goods, to the new Red Dead Ball they have recently introduced, in answer to the demand for a Ball which would possess all the life in it requisite for skillful batting, without the elasticity in its composition which makes it dangerous to field when batted hard or thrown swiftly.

Our new Ball is made of the best yarn, covering an ounce and a half of the best Unvulcanized Rubber,

5 ¼ OZ.

PECK & SNYDER
DEAD RED BALL

9¼ IN. CIRCUMFERENCE

and is of a Dark Red color, thereby getting rid of the objectionable dazzling whiteness of the ordinary ball which bothers fielders and batsmen on a Sunny Day in the early part of the contest.

"THE RED BALL"

Is used by all the Leading Clubs of the Metropolis in preference to all others, after one trial is had.

PECK & SNYDER,
Wholesale and Retail Dealers in Base Ball Players' Supplies.
126 NASSAU STREET, NEW YORK.

Price Lists of Base Ball Goods furnished free on Application.

Entered according to Act of Congress in the year 1870, by Peck & Snyder, in the Office of the Librarian of Congress, at Washington.

A century before Oakland owner Charlie Finley thought orange baseballs were a bright idea, the Peck & Snyder sporting goods company introduced its own colored baseball. But the "Dead Red Ball" was designed to make things easier on the players, not put more bodies in the seats.

petent persons." The home club chose one name, and the deal was done. Sometimes, though, the chosen man didn't show up, in which case the captains of the two teams picked another fellow to do the honors.

Not surprisingly, umpires didn't always have a perfect grasp of the rules, and this lack of professionalism gave weight to the next few generations' assessment of early baseball as crude and primitive: random selection of umpires, awkward rules poorly enforced and constantly changing, amateurs and professionals alike unable to sustain workable organizations. But 1870s baseball was far from primitive. The game still had a long way to go before it attained what Al Spalding in 1911 called "its present degree of perfection," but baseball in those early days was vigorous and adventurous as it hasn't been since. In that long-ago game of sidearm pitchers, bare-handed defenders and the fair-foul hit, we see a young, fresh and uninhibited version of our traditional, settled old sport. It's a lot like looking at a youthful photograph of someone we know quite well as an adult. We understand a little more about our friend, and the picture always makes us smile. ✪

Want a glimpse into baseball's past, perhaps an idea of what facing speedballers Jim Creighton and Asa Brainard was like? Get a seat behind the plate of a top-flight women's fast-pitch softball game and watch pitchers like Long Beach State's Ruby Flores (opposite).

Bob Ferguson

If they gave out awards for colorful nicknames, Bob Ferguson would have won more than his fair share. At various times throughout his long career, the outstanding infielder was known as "Death to Flying Things" for his fielding skill, as "Fighting Bob" for his hair-trigger temper and, in his umpiring days, as "Robber the Great" for his sometimes unpopular calls.

Death to Flying Things Ferguson was one of early baseball's ablest and most versatile figures. From 1864 to 1891 he served as a player, captain, manager, umpire and even league president. After pitching for the Frontiers of Brooklyn in 1864, the Brooklyn-born right-hander joined the Enterprise Club in 1865. Then in 1866 he jumped to the legendary Atlantics of Brooklyn, where he achieved fame as one of the game's best third basemen. Over the next 18 years, Ferguson also put in time at second base, shortstop and even behind the plate. He was less than a spectacular hitter, usually batting around .260, but he managed a career-high .351 with Chicago in 1878. He is credited with being the game's first switch hitter.

Ferguson, as his "Fighting Bob" moniker attests, had a legendary temper. "Turmoil was his middle name," noted one of his contemporaries, "and if he wasn't mixed up prominently in a scrap of some kind nearly every day, he would imagine he had not been of any use to the baseball fraternity and the community in general." Another writer described him as "aloof, conceited and stubborn." When he joined Philadelphia as player-manager in 1883, his teammates promptly revolted, and Ferguson was quickly relieved of his on-field authority. While umpiring a game between Baltimore and the Mutuals, Ferguson accused the Mutuals'

catcher of attempting to throw the game. When the player called Fighting Bob a liar, Ferguson grabbed a bat and broke the catcher's arm in two places. Ferguson could dish it out, and he could also take it. In 1881 with Troy he played five innings with a fractured wrist.

While Ferguson never won any popularity contests, he was known as a scrupulously honest player. As one writer noted, "Ferguson's primary contribution to baseball was his forthright character and unquestioned honesty in a time when many baseball players had low morals and were often the pawns of gamblers." Ferguson's spotless reputation helped him become elected president of the National Association in 1872.

The 5′ 9½″, 149-pounder ended his playing days in 1884 with Pittsburgh. In the same year he signed with New York but was forced to resign when several players who had played under him on former teams threatened to quit if he came aboard.

For the next six years Ferguson stayed in the game as an umpire. During times when umpires regularly feared for their lives and often had to be escorted out of stadiums by cordons of police, Ferguson was a notable exception. He seemed to fear no man, even that most dangerous of characters—the enraged fan. "Umping always came as easy to me as sleeping on a feather bed," he explained. "Never change a decision, never stop to talk with a man. Make 'em play ball and keep their mouths shut, and never fear but the people will be on your side and you'll be called king of umpires." The king of the early umpires, Robber the Great earned the respect of fans and players alike. Many of his rulings were used as guidelines and were later written into the baseball rulebook.

Before Bob Ferguson became one of the most colorful and controversial managers and umpires of the 1870s and 1880s, he made history as a player. On June 14, 1870, Ferguson drove in the tying run, then scored the winning run as Brooklyn broke Cincinnati's 92-game winning streak.

BOB
FERGUSON

Third Base, Second Base
Brooklyn Frontiers 1864
Brooklyn Enterprise 1865
Brooklyn Atlantics 1866–1870
National Association
New York Mutuals 1871
Brooklyn Atlantics 1872–1874
Hartford Dark Blues 1875
National League
Hartford Dark Blues 1876–1877
Chicago White Stockings 1878
Troy Trojans 1879–1882
Philadelphia Phillies 1883
American Association
Pittsburgh Alleghenys 1884

GAMES	821
AT-BATS	3,486
BATTING AVERAGE	
Career	.262
Season High	.351
HITS	
Career	912
Season High	96
RUNS	
Career	545
Season High	65
DOUBLES (NL, AA only)	
Career	76
Season High	15
TRIPLES (NL, AA only)	
Career	20
Season High	5
HOME RUNS (NL, AA only)	
Career	1
Season High	1
SLUGGING AVERAGE (NL, AA only)	
Career	.323
Season High	.405

Combined NA, NL and AA stats unless otherwise noted

OLD SHOES "FOR LUCK"

BOSTON

FAREWELL, DICK!
ORION CLUB

EUROPE

F. H. TAYLOR, Phila.

The Great Tour

Like soldiers off to war, the Boston Red Stockings and the Philadelphia Athletics were given a heroes' send-off before they steamed across the Atlantic in 1874 to bring the game of baseball to England. The New York Daily Graphic *gave its readers an impressive depiction of the historic event.*

America sent its best to England, and in 1874 that meant the Boston Red Stockings. Boston hit .327 as a team that season and lined up as follows: standing, from left, Cal McVey, .382; Al Spalding, .333; Deacon White, .321; Ross Barnes, .339; seated, from left, Jim O'Rourke, .344; Andy Leonard, .340; George Wright, .345; Harry Wright, .307; George Hall, .321; Harry Schafer, .265; Tommy Beals, .204.

During the baseball season of 1874, two of America's best ball-clubs, the Boston Red Stockings and the Philadelphia Athletics, set out for a tour of England. To modern eyes, it might seem strange that two teams crossed the Atlantic in the middle of summer to give demonstrations to an audience convinced that baseball was nothing more than a variation on the English children's game of rounders. But there were compelling reasons for such a tour.

At the time, Albert Spalding was a first-class pitcher for the champion Boston team. Years later, Spalding claimed to have promoted the tour himself, simply as a way to get to England. He couldn't afford such a venture himself, he said. But Spalding wasn't above a certain freedom with the facts. He went to England to set up the tour, all right, but he went at the request of Harry Wright, the man who conceived the idea of taking two baseball teams across the ocean. Wright, who had been born in England, wanted to demonstrate the American national sport in his native country. He was deeply proud of the fast and demanding game that he and others had created from town ball and the New York game of the Knickerbockers. And although he knew that baseball would never displace cricket in the hearts of Englishmen, he thought that it might at least gain a toehold in the country, like the one that association football—what we know as soccer—was gaining.

As to the time of year, the weather was the key. If you tried to play ball-games in England in any season other than summer, you faced the probability of chilly weather, rain and soggy grounds. Besides, teams in the National Association didn't have a formal schedule—each club made its own. Member clubs were expected to play a certain number of games against each other —ten in 1874—but they could play them any time from May 1 on.

In 1871 Spalding's image graced the cover of a scorecard sold at Boston's South End Grounds. Three years later he was Harry Wright's advance man on the Red Stockings' tour of England.

Future Hall of Famer Cap Anson was just 23 years old when he made the trip to England with the Athletics, but he was already one of the game's finest hitters. Anson hit .367 that season, playing three infield positions and the outfield.

After he got approval from the Red Stockings' directors, Wright sent Spalding off to England to set things up. He knew that the tall, handsome, well-mannered pitcher would make a good impression, and he thought that Spalding had good business sense, too.

Loaded down with letters of introduction, Spalding arrived in England in late January 1874 and immediately began to meet with "the leading men interested in out-door sports." He spoke to cricketers and journalists, was given a tour of London's best cricket grounds and was soon invited to discuss the proposed tour with the members of the aristocratic Marylebone Cricket Club. The MCC was the "home" of cricket world-wide, guardian of its traditions and arbiter of its rules. The place to stage baseball games in England was on cricket grounds, so if the tour was going to be a success, it had to have the blessing, if not the enthusiastic support, of the MCC.

As it turned out, the Marylebone members weren't especially interested in baseball, except as a curiosity. Realizing that "the cricket end was altogether most attractive from their viewpoint," young Al, like all great salesmen, adjusted his pitch to suit the customer. He told the Marylebone men that the American ballplayers could play cricket, too, and that they "might be able to do something in the national games of both countries." It wasn't long before one English journal announced that, "As most of the best cricketers in America are also the leading baseball players, they propose to play at both games." There was one minor problem: Harry and George Wright were fine cricketers, and Dick McBride of the Athletics had some experience at the game, but precious few of the other ballplayers on either the Boston or the Philadelphia team—Spalding

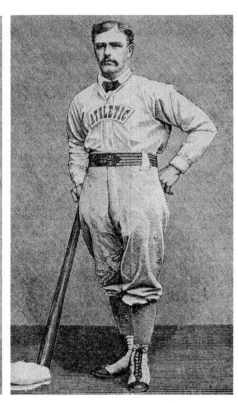

The Red Stockings may have been the best team in the National Association in 1874, but their traveling partners—the Philadelphia Athletics—were the heaviest hitters, with a .331 team batting average. Three of the best were outfielder John McMullin (left), .387, infielder Mike McGeary (center), .362, and catcher John Clapp (right), .331.

included—knew the basics of the English game. So much for their being "the best cricketers in America."

Spalding, of course, was simply doing what he had to do to close his sale. He'd worry about the details later. In the meantime, he kept everybody happy—at least temporarily. He wrote home to tell Wright that "there is a strong desire to see first-class baseball matches." He assured his manager that the English were eager to learn the fine points of our national game and that a baseball tour would make at least enough money to cover expenses.

Spalding got the go-ahead from the MCC, and he plunged forward, setting up a schedule for the tour. To help him, he signed up Charles Alcock as the tour's agent. Alcock was secretary of the Surrey cricket club, the cricket editor of the *London Sportsman* and, according to Spalding, "the recognized cricket authority of England"—a sort of cricketeering Henry Chadwick.

By telling Wright and Alcock what they wanted to hear, Spalding misled them both: Wright believed that his dream of demonstrating baseball to an interested English audience—and making a little money on the deal—was about to come true; Alcock was anticipating a series of grand international cricket matches, interspersed with occasional baseball exhibitions.

Back home, Wright and his allies had been trying to sell the idea on this side of the Atlantic. Quite apart from the financial risks, some worried about the effect of two of the best teams in the National Association simply taking off in the middle of the season. In early March the *Boston Herald* reminded readers of the NA's peculiar schedule: "Those who attended the matches on the Boston grounds are aware that during the months of July and August com-

Dick McBride (left) was the Athletics' ace in 1874 with a 33–22 mark. He got a lot of help from the bats of infielders Ezra Sutton (center), .346, and Wes Fisler (right), .383.

paratively few matches are played there, and the same is the case in all parts of the country. In five weeks of those months last year the Athletic club did not play a single match, and a large portion of that time the Boston nine was away from home and playing with amateur clubs." The public was assured that "the absence of the nine will not effect the number of championship games to be played in this city this year." Furthermore, "during the time in which the Boston nine are away interesting matches will be played here by other clubs." And the paper—nothing if not partisan—concluded that Athletics president James Ferguson "has entered heartily into the measure," and that the tour "can be made successful if the chronic croakers will take a back seat and the true friends come forward and lend a helping hand." The croakers moved quickly to the rear, and the Great Baseball—and cricket —Tour was on.

Once the decision was made firm, even the croakers seemed pleased with the two teams that were making the trip. It would never do to send a bunch of ruffians, drunkards or cheats on tour, and the Red Stockings and Athletics would reflect honor on their country and their sport if anyone could. As one newspaper put it, "the players who are going over are gentlemen whose conduct will never throw discredit upon the city they represent."

Wright may not have been worried about the players' conduct, but he was deeply concerned about how they would look on a cricket pitch. Spalding later claimed that almost none of the players had ever even seen a cricket match before they played one in England, but, in fact, Harry Wright did his best to teach them the rudiments before they left. In May the two teams par-

The Red Stockings were baseball's most marketable commodity in the United States in 1874, and the two-time defending NA champs appeared on everything from tobacco labels (right) to ads for whiskey. But on the other side of the Atlantic, they—and their game—were virtual unknowns.

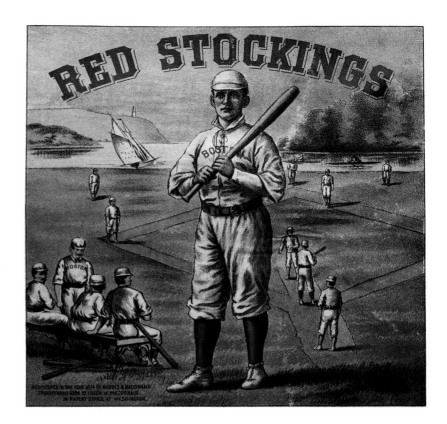

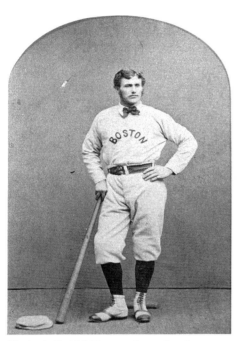

Boston's Cal McVey may have played baseball across more time zones than any other player of his era. Two years after he made the trip to England, he made Chicago his home base. Four years later he went to California and organized and managed clubs in Oakland, Hanford and San Diego.

ticipated in a match against Philadelphia's Young America Cricket Club. George Wright and Dick McBride both looked like reasonable cricketers, and Harry was an experienced bowler. These three no doubt tried to coach the other players in basic techniques, but cricket is a complex and subtle sport. Even great athletes like Spalding, Al Reach and Adrian Anson couldn't pick it up in a day.

The tour left Philadelphia on Thursday, July 16, sailing down the Delaware on the American Line steamer *Ohio*. The traveling party was given a terrific send-off, which didn't end when the ship pulled away from the dock. Friends and relatives climbed on board to continue the party as the *Ohio* chugged toward open ocean. McClurg's Liberty Cornet Band played dance music, and a Philadelphia paper reported that "it was clearly demonstrated that some, if not all, of the players understood the 'glide' as well as sliding in on a stolen run."

Unfortunately, such high spirits weren't as evident on the team's arrival in England. They landed in Liverpool and immediately started complaining. Turnout for their first baseball game, on July 30, was scant. There had been, they felt, "a complete failure to stir up interest, which may be attributed to a sparing use of printer's ink." They were right. Alcock hadn't promoted the baseball games, only the cricket matches.

Nonetheless, the game was welcomed politely by the local press. After the first game, which the Athletics won, 14–11, the *Liverpool Post* wrote that "Base-ball must be regarded as an improvement on the old 'rounders,' and although it is scarcely likely to supersede the favourite game of our summer seasons in England, yet it is undoubtedly a splendid means for exercising the

In the smoking-room.

The second day out.

Playing shuffle board.

The rush for dinner.

On deck.

Tossing the ring.

limbs and muscles, and sharpening the perception and judgment of those who may make it a pastime; and it may possibly attain some considerable popularity before our American friends return to their native country."

After that too-optimistic opening, the *Post* went on to praise the ball-players' fielding and throwing—an appreciation that was to become almost universal while the Americans were in England. But the paper didn't quite approve of another aspect of the American game: "Cries of 'Hurry on,' 'What are you doing?' and so forth, are frequently raised by the chief and echoed on all sides by those who are personally interested in the contest. This, on a cricket field, would, of course, not be permitted during a first-class match." Harrumph.

The tourists traveled to London for their first cricket match against the Marylebone Cricket Club on August 3 at Lord's, the Yankee Stadium of the sport. Before the match, they tried once again to get the hang of the game. It was a disaster. As Spalding tells it, "We had hardly begun when [Alcock] came up to me and said: 'For Heaven's sake, Spalding, what are your men trying to do?' I explained that they were just engaging in a little preliminary practice. 'But, man, alive,' he expostulated, 'that isn't cricket. Why, you led me to suppose that your fellows were cricketers as well as ball players, and here have I been filling the London papers with assurances of close matches. Why, Spalding, your men don't know the rudiments of the game.' "

"We are not much in practice, but we are great in matches," Spalding replied. He was right. The Americans went on to beat Marylebone, and to compile a total of four wins and three draws—called because of weather— while in England. Spalding and the American press never stopped crowing about the record, but it was actually a farce. In the first place, the Americans

Continued on page 164

Although the great tour suffered from a lack of publicity in England, no such problem existed on the west side of the Atlantic. The activities of America's baseball ambassadors were reported in vivid detail (above), and the press seemed generally pleased with their behavior. The Rockford Register *commended the players for behaving like "good boys when three to four thousand miles away from their mothers."*

Jefferson Street Grounds

The teams have come and gone—mostly gone—but more than a century after the first pitch was ever thrown there, they're still playing baseball at 27th and Jefferson Streets in Philadelphia. Nowadays the field hosts recreation league baseball, but on a cloudy afternoon in April 1876, Jefferson Street Grounds played host to the first game in the history of the National League.

The game featured two traditional powerhouses of the then-defunct National Association—the Boston Red Stockings and the Philadelphia Athletics. The teams had finished 1–2 in the 1875 NA standings, but as the NL's inaugural season opened they were hurting. Boston had lost its four best players—Al Spalding, Cal McVey, Deacon White and Ross Barnes—to Chicago, while the Athletics were without staff ace Dick McBride, who went 44–14 in 1875. Still, a crowd of about 3,000 showed up that Saturday to watch a game that featured 26 errors and took two hours and five minutes to play. Boston scored twice in the ninth to take a 6–5 win.

By 1876 Jefferson Street Grounds had seen its share of fine baseball. The Athletics won the pennant in 1871, the National Association's first season, and were consistently in the first division. The park featured the customary 500-foot distance to center field but narrowed considerably toward the foul lines. The only real grandstand was along the first-base line, but according to one reporter the park's press facilities were first-rate, "placed directly back of the catcher, and sufficiently elevated to be out of the reach of strong foul balls that may chance their way."

But the Athletics didn't even finish the season in 1876, and Jefferson Street Grounds was without major league baseball until 1883, when Philadelphia got an American Association franchise. The field was spruced up, and, led by Harry Stovey's 14 home runs and Bobby Mathews' 30 wins, the team brought a second pennant to Jefferson Street Grounds. They didn't win another pennant before the American Association disbanded in 1891, but they turned in their fair share of highlights. Stovey won five home run titles, including a high of 19 homers in 1889. But perhaps Jefferson Street Grounds should be remembered as a pitcher's park. Of the 15 no-hitters thrown in the American Association's ten-year history, four were thrown by Philadelphia pitchers at their home park. Al Atkinson threw no-hitters in 1884 and 1886, then in 1888 Ed Seward and Gus Weyhing tossed no-hitters just five days apart.

Jefferson Street Grounds

Jefferson and 27th Streets
Philadelphia, Pennsylvania

Built 1871

Philadelphia Athletics, NA
1871–1875
Philadelphia White Stockings, NA
1873–1875

Philadelphia Athletics, NL
1876
Philadelphia Athletics, AA
1883–1891

Style
Wooden

With the Civil War over in 1865, Americans could get back to more leisurely pursuits, like taking in a ballgame. In Philadelphia the best baseball was played at Jefferson Street Grounds, where on October 30 the Brooklyn Atlantics beat the Philadelphia Athletics, 21–15 (above). It was Brooklyn's 16th win of the season without a loss.

In the only known surviving photo from the great tour, the Red Stockings and Athletics posed at the Greyhound Club in Richmond, Surrey, where the two teams battled each other in England's national game, cricket.

Second baseman Ross Barnes was among the most precious cargo the Red Stockings took to England. Barnes hit above .400 in both 1872 and 1873, and his outstanding fielding made him, in Al Spalding's opinion, "one of the best all around players the game has produced."

were allowed to play 18 and sometimes 22 men against English teams of 11—the usual number—12 or 13. And in the second place, the ballplayers played in a way that simply wasn't "cricket."

With the exception of McBride and the two Wrights, the ballplayers simply hacked away at the ball when they were at bat. This produced some long hits and lots of runs, but failed to impress the British, to whom style was at least as important as the result. They called the American batting "blind slogging."

Today, big-time cricket has given up many of the old-fashioned niceties, but as recently as the 1930s there was serious debate over something called "body-line bowling," the equivalent of the brushback pitch. It was considered inappropriate, unsportsmanlike, ungentlemanly, not good for the game—"not cricket." The fact that it was effective and within the rules didn't matter.

Needless to say, this sort of reasoning didn't make an impression on Spalding or his teammates. They continued to accept their advantage in numbers, to hack away and to celebrate victories that the English considered meaningless. The result was that British newspapers, expecting a serious cricket tour, stopped covering the matches. And the public, who might have turned out to watch true American cricket, never showed up. Weren't they interested in seeing America's national game? Well, no. And despite what Spalding had told Wright, they never had been.

The tour continued, although Wright must have known after the first week that it was going to be a financial disaster. His records show that he did most of the bowling in the seven cricket matches Alcock had scheduled. His brother George was acclaimed as both the most graceful and the most effec-

5' 9½" 173 lbs.
BR TR

b 3/1/1852
d 7/10/1935

PAUL HINES
Outfield

On May 8, 1878, in the eighth inning of a close game, Providence center fielder Paul Hines made a play that kept baseball pundits debating for years. The issue was whether he had completed an unassisted triple play, becoming the first National Leaguer to do so.

The play Hines did make was amazing, but it was not an unassisted triple play. With no outs and runners on second and third, Boston's John Burdock hit a twisting fly that appeared certain to drop safely behind the shortstop. The runners broke for home, but the speedy Hines made a great catch on the run. His momentum carried him to third, where he tagged the bag, then threw to second baseman Charlie Sweasy to complete the triple play. Some reports said both runners had rounded third and credited Hines with all three outs. Hines was willing to take the credit, but other observers recorded the play as two putouts and an assist.

Hines was a hustling competitor. From 1872 to 1891, the Washington, D.C., native played for eight teams in three leagues, batted .301 and led two clubs to three NL championships. In 1878 Hines' .358 average, four homers and 50 RBI made him the first-ever winner of the NL's triple crown.

Hines was invited to be the first person to catch a ball dropped from the top of the Washington Monument when it was completed in 1884, but he thought the publicity stunt was too risky. "I plan to live a long time," he said, "and that's no way to go about it."

tive cricketer among the Americans. In baseball, Boston won eight, Philadelphia, six. George was outstanding there, too, leading all hitters over the 14 games.

Some early raves about baseball appeared in the English press, at least one of which was probably written by Henry Chadwick. By and large, though, while journalists recognized the advantages of a game that could be played in two hours, they viewed baseball condescendingly: "The game is a somewhat simple one," one writer reported, "without the number of subtleties which distinguish and make incomprehensible cricket or tennis."

Still, the "travelling ball tossers" were constantly praised for their skills in the field, which they showed off equally well in cricket matches and baseball games. "The admirable part of the play had all through been the fielding," wrote the *London Post* after that first bizarre cricket match. "Nothing hit up in the air escaped. The accuracy of the catching would have made many a slow bowler envious of the pairs of hands. But the accuracy and skill of the catching was surpassed by the wonderful precision of the throwing. A moment to look, a moment to get the proper equilibrium, and then the ball is hurled 'sharp and low' quite straight to the base-man's hands. No fumbling half-volleys, no wide throws. So accurate was it that the exclamations of many a cricketer present was—With such throwing who would not be a wicket-keeper?"

The American visitors played out the tour, hopping over to Dublin for their final pair of baseball games and their last cricket match. Then they headed home, braving a rough passage and arriving back on September 10.

The architecture may have been slightly different, but the game was the same as the Red Stockings and Athletics battled it out on the ballfields of England. Still, the British press was only mildly impressed. The London Telegraph *reported that "few of the youth of Great Britain will desert cricket with its dignity, manliness and system for a rushing, helter-skelter game."*

Wright didn't try to hide the fact that the trip had been a financial flop. But to keep the croakers at bay, friendly journalists waxed ecstatic over the American cricket victories. They assured their readers that the British had been taught to respect baseball as a great sport in its own right. Why Americans cared what the English thought might be difficult for us to understand today. But they did—they cared obsessively. The *Brooklyn Eagle* even went so far as to state that the tour of England made 1874 "the year in which base ball was for the first time fully recognized and established as the National Game of America."

Losses came to about $3,000. With foresight, the directors of the two clubs had had the players sign contracts before they departed that called for pay cuts if the tour lost money. Needless to say, the players weren't happy with the result. Adrian Anson later wrote that the players had gone to England as "argonauts" but "brought back but little of the golden fleece."

When they got home, the Red Stockings and the Athletics simply picked up their National Association games where they'd left off. Boston kept its promise to play its full quota of games, and it ran away with the pennant for the third year in a row. The Athletics finished third, with the Mutuals tucked in between. But the championship race was judged by almost everyone to have been the second most important baseball event of the year. The tour was first.

And the tour, as silly as it seems today, *was* important. Not because it showed that Americans could play cricket—they couldn't—or because it somehow proved to the English that baseball was a good game—it didn't—

but because it was a watershed in the business of the game. It took men of foresight, like Wright and Spalding, to realize how important promotion was in ensuring the future of baseball.

The tour of 1874 was recognized at the time as Wright's baby. He was honored for it by his peers and in the pages of dozens of newspapers. Eventually, though, the tour came to be thought of as Spalding's. He'd negotiated the schedule, after all. He'd dealt with the "Dooks" abroad. He'd made the contacts with the press. Spalding, in a way, took credit for the 1874 tour away from Wright, mirroring the change in who controlled the game: away from business*like* professional sportsmen to professional business*men*. Harry Wright was business*like*—careful in his dealings, fastidious in keeping records. Al Spalding, on the other hand, was a born business*man*—a promoter, a salesman, a player of angles—the sort of fellow who could capitalize on his skills at the game and amass a fortune.

Wright had thought of the trip to England, but Spalding had used gall and wild promises to make it a reality. The next year, Spalding cut himself a deal to leave Wright's Red Stockings and go to Chicago. The deal meant not only a much larger salary, but also a piece of the recuperating White Stockings. Shortly thereafter, Spalding threw in with the businessmen who created the National League. Soon enough, he started his own successful sporting goods business. Harry Wright's influence, based mainly on force of character, was fading. Al Spalding, the promoter and money man, was on his way to becoming the dominant figure in the business of baseball for the rest of the 19th century. ◑

Famed Lord's Cricket Grounds in the St. John's Wood section of London was transformed into a baseball field in 1874 for a game between the Red Stockings and the Athletics, as a large and curious crowd looked on.

Ross Barnes

From Rogers Hornsby to Ryne Sandberg, baseball's history has been jammed with brilliant second basemen, players who starred at the plate, in the field and on the basepaths. Ross Barnes was the prototype.

Barnes was one of baseball's first true superstars, the kind of player who not only helped his teams win games, but helped shape the game itself. He was a master of the fair-foul hit, in which the batter slaps the ball so that it bounces in fair territory then quickly crosses into foul territory between home and the base. The ball was still playable under existing rules, and the fair-foul hit was almost impossible to defend against. The hit helped Barnes win three batting titles; he was so good at the fair-foul hit that it was ruled illegal in 1877, establishing the distinction between a fair and a foul ball that still exists today.

Barnes was also one of the first players to adjust his position in the field according to who was at bat, a tactic we take for granted in today's game, but one that was downright prescient in the 1870s. Of Barnes' fielding, the *New York Clipper* wrote: "One point of excellence was his shrewd judgment in covering the infield according to his batsman; one time playing almost back of first base, then at short right field, and then back of second base. In fact, he was a base-playing strategist, and in this specialty he had no equal."

Barnes joined the Forest Citys of Rockford, Illinois, at 16, along with future Hall of Famer Al Spalding. Barnes and Spalding were teammates for the next 11 years, and in 1871 they signed with Harry Wright to play for baseball's first superteam,

the Boston Red Stockings of the National Association. Barnes and shortstop George Wright were the team's one-two hitters and a hot double play combination, and they helped lead Boston to four straight NA pennants from 1872 to 1875. Barnes won two NA batting titles and hit .379 in his five years with the team.

In 1876 Barnes jumped—along with teammates Cal McVey and Deacon White—to Spalding's new team, the Chicago White Stockings of the National League. He took the new league by storm, and with his .429 average became the first player ever to win batting titles in two leagues. He also hit the NL's first home run, and led the league with 138 hits, 21 doubles, 14 triples, 20 walks, a .590 slugging percentage and a remarkable 126 runs scored in just 66 games. Chicago went 52–14 to win the NL's inaugural pennant, while Harry Wright's Red Stockings foundered in fourth place.

The next season, however, Barnes' average sank to .272. Some say it was because his patented fair-foul hit was illegal and he couldn't adjust; others attribute it to an ailment that kept him out of all but 22 games that season, but in any case he never regained his previous form. Barnes hit .266 for Cincinnati in 1879 and .271 for Boston in 1881, his final two seasons in the majors.

In just nine seasons as a professional, the 5′ 8½″, 145-pound second baseman helped set the standard for triple-threat ballplayers with his bat, his speed and a great pair of hands. His obituary in the 1916 *Spalding's Official Base Ball Guide* put it best: "He was almost Base Ball perfect in everything."

WARREN,

289 Washington St.
Boston.

HEALD,

Even without a glove, second baseman Ross Barnes made the tough plays look easy. Famous for winning the National League's first batting title by a margin of more than 60 points, he also led NL second basemen with a .910 fielding percentage that season.

ROSS
BARNES

Infield
Rockford Forest Citys 1866–1870
National Association
Boston Red Stockings 1871–1875
National League
Chicago White Stockings 1876–1877
Cincinnati Red Stockings 1879
Boston Red Stockings 1881
International Association
London, Ontario, Tecumsehs 1878

GAMES	**542**
AT-BATS	**2,627**
BATTING AVERAGE	
Career	**.346**
Season High	**.429**
HITS	
Career	**909**
Season High	**148**
RUNS	
Career	**726**
Season High	**126**
DOUBLES (NL only)	
Career	**45**
Season High	**21**
TRIPLES (NL only)	
Career	**17**
Season High	**14**
HOME RUNS (NL only)	
Career	**2**
Season High	**1**
SLUGGING AVERAGE (NL only)	
Career	**.401**
Season High	**.590**
RUNS BATTED IN (NL only)	
Career	**111**
Season High	**59**

Combined NA, NL and IA stats unless otherwise noted

A Major Undertaking

The year of the nation's much-celebrated centennial, the year George Armstrong Custer's 7th Cavalry perished at Little Bighorn, was also the year that American baseball gave birth to its first major league. In 1876, 30 years after the Knickerbockers wrote the first rulebook, 18 years after early amateur clubs put together the first National Association, seven years after the Cincinnati Red Stockings introduced well-drilled, salaried players, professional baseball finally established itself as a serious business. And it took a serious businessman to make it happen.

In June 1875 the Chicago White Stockings elected stockholder William A. Hulbert president of the club. The White Stockings had been back in the National Association since 1874, but they had never really recovered from the Great Fire of 1871 or the blaze of 1874. Hulbert, a 42-year-old coal merchant and self-made man, immediately took steps toward turning the White Stockings into baseball's best team: he raided Harry Wright's Boston Red Stockings. During the 1875 season, while Albert Spalding was pitching the Red Stockings to yet another NA pennant, Hulbert secretly met with the ambitious young ballplayer. He offered Spalding not just more money, but the job of team manager and a financial interest in the club. Never one to miss a chance, Spalding agreed to move to Chicago for the 1876 season.

Then Hulbert and Spalding went to work on the remaining core of the Boston team. Soon they had secret commitments from Ross Barnes, Cal

In order to cement his stewardship of the new National League, White Stockings president William Hulbert needed a pennant in the league's first year. He got it, as the White Stockings (opposite) finished 52–14, six games ahead of St. Louis.

Buying stock in the Louisville Grays in 1876 (right) looked like a pretty sound investment, as the Grays featured Jim Devlin, one of the National League's finest pitchers. But in 1877 Devlin and three of his teammates were kicked out of baseball for fixing games, and the team disbanded. William Hulbert (below) was the driving force behind the NL and was vigilant in his efforts to keep the new league free of the corruption that had plagued the National Association.

McVey and Jim "Deacon" White. But word eventually leaked out that "the Big Four" were planning to jump to Chicago. Wright was not pleased, and fans worried that the four players might not play their best for the remainder of the season and that the controversy would undermine the Red Stockings' impressive teamwork. True professionals that they were, Spalding, Barnes, McVey and White played well all season, and Boston, with a record of 71–8, once again dominated the NA in 1875. Their closest competitors, the Philadelphia Athletics, were 53–20. In Philadelphia, Hulbert spotted another player whom he wanted, and he soon signed Adrian "Cap" Anson, who eventually became the first player to collect 3,000 big-league hits.

This kind of piracy wasn't unheard of in the National Association, but everyone knew it could lead to the suspension of the players involved. This wouldn't be good for Chicago baseball, and it would be even worse for the careers of Spalding and his three teammates. Hulbert responded to this threat in typical style. "You boys are bigger than the Association," he assured his new players.

"Spalding," he is reported to have said to his new lieutenant, "I have a scheme. Let us anticipate the Eastern cusses and organize a new association before the March meeting, and then see who will do the expelling." Hulbert's timing was perfect. The NA was weak and tottering, riddled with corruption and instability. By taking the initiative, Hulbert could also head off any disciplinary measures suggested by the eastern clubs that dominated the NA. He already had some ideas about the way professional baseball should be run. He'd been talking to Harry Wright. Although Wright hadn't liked losing four of his best players, he had long been critical of the NA and he feared for the future of the professional game. During 1875 he and Hulbert corresponded

In 1867 Adrian Anson (standing, far right) played second base for the Iowa state champion Marshalltown team, and he went on to become one of the National League's first superstars, hitting over .300 twenty times in his 22-year career with Chicago.

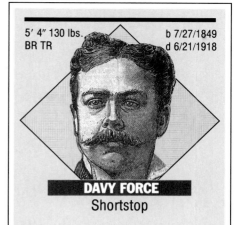

5′ 4″ 130 lbs.
BR TR

b 7/27/1849
d 6/21/1918

DAVY FORCE
Shortstop

Some players slug their way into baseball stardom. Others gain fame with their arms, their gloves or their tactical genius. Davy Force, although a great shortstop and second baseman for 15 years, won his niche in baseball history with a pen.

In 1874 Force had a solid year with the Chicago White Stockings. But since contracts had no reserve clause, players frequently signed with more than one team, and Force felt free both to renew his contract with Chicago *and* to sign with the Philadelphia Athletics. The Chicago contract was signed first, but when a Philadelphian became president of the National Association, he had the league's judiciary committee award Force to the Athletics. Chicago owner William Hulbert, already upset with lax NA procedures, vowed to destroy the NA. By 1876 the NA was no more, Hulbert was the father of the National League and Force was playing for Philadelphia—in the NL.

On the field, Force had "the same awkward grace" as Hall of Famer Honus Wagner, according to sportswriter Francis Richter, who ranked Force second only to George Wright among shortstops of the era. In his best year at the plate, 1872, Force hit .412, and for the next three years, his season average never dropped below .302.

Force played for several NL teams before retiring in 1886. He hit only .211 over ten seasons, but his glove made him a standout and he led the NL six times in fielding percentage.

about what steps were needed to put the game on a solid footing, and a number of the proposals that Hulbert ultimately included in the draft constitution of his new league were first voiced by Harry Wright.

Hulbert began his scheme by asking a friendly journalist to float a trial balloon. In October 1875 Louis Meacham of the *Chicago Tribune* published a proposal for reorganizing the NA that contained four main elements. The first was that all clubs should be backed by financially responsible organizations; the association's teams must be run by businessmen, not dilettantes. The second element was that no clubs from cities with populations under 100,000 should be allowed. Teams in smaller cities simply couldn't sell enough tickets to make money—or to make road trips worthwhile for other teams. The article recommended that an exception be made for Hartford, which had demonstrated good management and stability. Third, there should be no more than one club in each city competing in the association. Why split the big-league gate among two or three teams? The final point suggested that each team be required to demonstrate good faith by depositing $1,000 to $1,500 in an escrow account before the season opened. Hulbert and his colleagues believed that undercapitalization was a symptom of poor management; it had caused many problems over the years, forcing teams to cancel road trips or to drop out during the season.

These proposals meant real changes: two of the three teams in Philadelphia would have to go, and smaller cities like New Haven, which was already planning to field an NA team in 1876, would be disqualified. Clearly, the NA could not implement these radical changes, even if it reorganized. But the truth was that Hulbert was not interested in

Continued on page 175

The Louisville Scandal

In August of 1877 the Louisville Grays—led by ace pitcher Jim Devlin and slugging outfielder George Hall—were on the verge of clinching the NL pennant. Then suddenly their dominance turned into incompetence. They began to lose. After they lost eight games in a row, the Louisville press and fans knew the losses were more than a slump. The fix was in.

All four players implicated in the scandal —Devlin, Hall, infielders Al Nichols and Bill Craver —had reputations for consorting with gamblers. The scheme to throw the pennant may have been George Hall's idea, because when Grays third baseman Bill Hague came down with a case of the boils midway through the season, Hall suggested to manager Jack Chapman that they bring in Nichols to fill out the roster. There were probably better third basemen than Nichols available—he had hit just .179 with New York the previous year—but none who had better connections with New York gamblers.

When Louisville lost two games to Hartford because of poor pitching by Devlin and errors by Hall and Craver, the stench was unmistakable. Club vice president Charles Chase had already received anonymous warnings that gamblers were betting heavily on the Grays to lose, and he was suspicious of the inordinate number of telegrams Nichols received in each town Louisville played. Chase grilled Devlin, who admitted he had thrown some exhibition games but not regular season NL contests. Hall, thinking Devlin had already spilled the beans about the pennant race, confessed to fixing the Grays' games and named Nichols as the ringleader. Chase requested permission to examine all telegrams received by the suspected Grays. Craver refused and was expelled from the team. Under the threat of expulsion, the other players complied. The telegrams contained coded words and messages, including the word *sash,* which meant a fixed game. The other three were expelled from the team, and at the league's winter meeting, the governing board banned the four conspirators from the NL for life.

In the years that followed there were a number of attempts to assign responsibility for the scandal. One scenario is that Hall and Nichols persuaded Devlin to throw a meaningless exhibition game for $100 and then forced him to throw other games without reward by threatening to expose his one day of dirty work.

The players were to some degree driven by circumstances to seek other income. A baseball player's life was often wretched, particularly on the road, and to make matters worse, the shakily financed Louisville club had been failing to make regular salary payments. But the Louisville scandal represented the first time that the ruling magnates of baseball used their authority to punish players for going in the tank. Throughout the five years of NA play, the only things as certain as gambling's pervasive influence were the league's toothless regulations and token condemnations. So in just the second season of the National League, baseball fans first greeted news of this scandal with impassive resignation. They were soon surprised to find that the new league planned to take firm and severe action. Finally, organized baseball had come to understand the link between the success of baseball as a business and the preservation of the game's integrity.

J. S. Thompson & Co., Printers, Times Building, 88 Fifth Avenue, Chicago.

reorganization. Through his mouthpiece, Meacham, Hulbert was proposing an entirely new organization.

One other thing: Hulbert wanted no more of an association dominated by easterners. He had once told Spalding, "I would rather be a lamp-post in Chicago than a millionaire in another city." And because he knew that other men in "the West" would agree, he began selling his idea in his own neighborhood first. Soon after the article in the *Tribune* appeared, Hulbert, Spalding and Meacham traveled to St. Louis for secret conferences with Charles Fowle, president of the NA St. Louis club. They brought with them a rough draft of a new constitution based on the proposals in Meacham's article, which was whipped into shape by St. Louis attorney Campbell Orrick Bishop, a vice-president of the NA and a member of its judiciary committee. Fowle liked the plan.

With St. Louis behind them, the Chicagoans arranged a meeting with the directors of the Louisville and Cincinnati clubs on December 17, 1875. When they were through, they had, as Hulbert wrote, "four powerful clubs welded together." It was time to tackle the East. They were in a position to pick and choose, and they chose what they considered to be the four strongest and most stable teams: Boston, the Mutuals of New York, the Philadelphia Athletics and the Hartford Grays. On January 23, 1876, Hulbert and Fowle sent copies of a letter to the eastern clubs' directors:

Gentlemen:
The undersigned have been appointed by the Chicago, Cincinnati, Louisville and St. Louis clubs, a committee to confer with you on matters of interest to the game at large, with a special

With the best players from the four-time NA champion Boston Red Stockings in tow, the Chicago White Stockings were the dominant team in the National League's inaugural season. Chicago outscored its opponents by an average of 9.5 to 3.9 runs per game, and had eight .300-plus hitters in the starting lineup.

5' 7" 142 lbs.
BL
b 6/22/1849
d 6/11/1923

GEORGE HALL
Outfield

Offering his talent to the highest bidder came naturally to George Hall, and the Brooklyn-raised outfielder had a considerable amount of talent to offer. He hit .301 in five years of NA play, but truly came into his own in 1876—the NL's maiden year—when he hit .366 and became the league's first home run champion, knocking an awesome total of five long balls.

Hall had gone to the Brooklyn Atlantics in 1870. The Atlantics beat the undefeated Cincinnati Red Stockings that year, but Hall took a hint from the Cincinnati team: paid ballplayers and winning go hand in hand. So when Brooklyn decided to reorganize as an amateur team the following year, Hall went off to play center field for the professional Washington (D.C.) Olympics. He jumped to another team again in 1872. When the Olympics were unable to finance the payroll, Hall joined the Lord Baltimores for two seasons in which he hit .300 and .320.

Hall may well have had friends among baseball's confidence men before he went to Philadelphia to play with the Athletics in 1875 and 1876. But in a town where baseball betting pools were conducted openly at games, he solidified his relationship with some of the game's worst elements. He confessed to throwing games while with the Louisville Grays in 1877. That winter the NL banned him from league play for life.

In 1876 the Chicago White Stockings not only ran off with the NL's first pennant, they did it in style. The Chicago Evening Journal *reported that "every man on the club has shown himself to be a gentleman as well as a ball player."*

reference to the reformation of existing abuses, and the formation of a new association, and we are clothed with full authority in writing from the above-named clubs to bind them to any arrangement we may make with you. We therefore invite your club to send a representative, clothed with like authority, to meet us at the Grand Central hotel, in the city of New York, on Wednesday, the second day of February next, at 12 M. After careful consideration of the needs of the professional clubs, the organizations we represent are of the firm belief that existing circumstances demand prompt and vigorous action by those who are the natural sponsors of the game. It is the earnest recommendation of our constituents that all past troubles and differences be ignored and forgotten, and that the conference we propose shall be a calm, friendly and deliberate discussion, looking solely to the general good of the clubs who are calculated to give character and permanency to the game. We are confident that the propositions we have to submit will meet with your approval and support, and we shall be pleased to meet you at the time and place above mentioned.

Yours respectfully,
W.A. HULBERT
CHAS. A. FOWLE

The press paid no attention whatsoever to Hulbert's maneuverings, and there were no reporters sniffing around on the appointed day, so we don't know all of what went on at the meeting. It's likely, though, that at least some

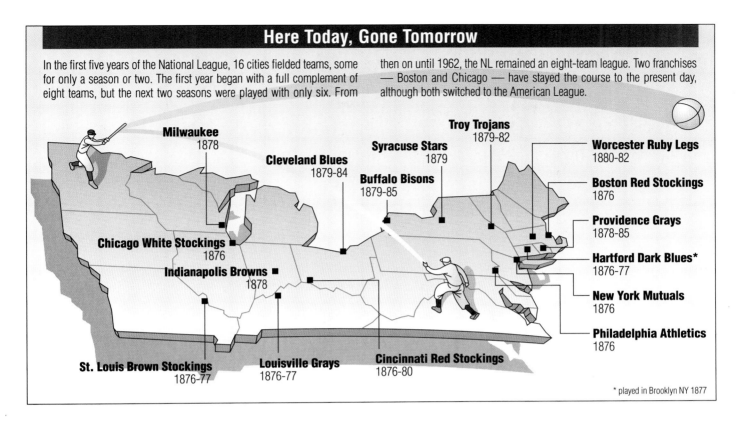

Here Today, Gone Tomorrow

In the first five years of the National League, 16 cities fielded teams, some for only a season or two. The first year began with a full complement of eight teams, but the next two seasons were played with only six. From then on until 1962, the NL remained an eight-team league. Two franchises — Boston and Chicago — have stayed the course to the present day, although both switched to the American League.

Milwaukee 1878

Cleveland Blues 1879-84

Troy Trojans 1879-82

Syracuse Stars 1879

Buffalo Bisons 1879-85

Worcester Ruby Legs 1880-82

Boston Red Stockings 1876

Chicago White Stockings 1876

Providence Grays 1878-85

Indianapolis Browns 1878

Hartford Dark Blues* 1876-77

New York Mutuals 1876

Philadelphia Athletics 1876

St. Louis Brown Stockings 1876-77

Louisville Grays 1876-77

Cincinnati Red Stockings 1876-80

* played in Brooklyn NY 1877

of the invited directors were less than thrilled to be summoned by these two pushy westerners—one of whom had just stolen five of the best players in the East. They certainly weren't ready for Hulbert's plea that they all forgive and forget. According to legend, they were so hostile that Hulbert locked them in the hotel room, pocketed the key and announced that he wasn't going to let anyone out until they'd come to an agreement. This makes good drama, but it almost certainly didn't happen. Hulbert probably got them to stay the same way he got them to show up in the first place: he had a good idea that might work to their advantage.

By late evening on February 2, 1876, the National Association was, for all intents and purposes, dead. The National League had been born. Under the new constitution, member clubs owned exclusive rights to National League baseball in their cities. There would be no profitless trips to small cities with small crowds: no city with a population under 75,000 could be awarded a team. Furthermore, the league controlled membership decisions; even if a new club met all the criteria, it could be denied membership if two league clubs blackballed it.

The newspapers didn't report on the great coup until three days later, and the first stories focused on the fact that the Philadelphia Phillies had been cut out of the new league in favor of the Athletics. Hulbert had indeed seen who would do the expelling.

The real story, though, lay in the name of the new league. The National Association of Professional Baseball *Players* had been succeeded by the National League of Professional Baseball *Clubs*. The shift in power from the players to the clubs was a real revolution in the history of the game. From this point on, the sport was going to be run for the benefit

The newly formed National League turned
the focus of baseball's ever-evolving set of
rules toward the role of the umpire in its first
few years. In 1877 the league chose "three
gentlemen of repute" in each NL city to
provide a pool from which the visiting team
would select one. In 1878 umpires became
pros at $5 a game.

MORGAN G. BULKELEY

*Morgan Bulkeley was an appropriate choice
for president of the national pastime's first
major league. Bulkeley's ancestors had come
over on the* Mayflower, *he had fought for the
Union in the Civil War and he was a captain
of the insurance industry. After his one-year
tenure as NL president, he worked his way
up the political ladder from mayor of Hartford
to governor of Connecticut to U.S. senator.*

of the businessmen who owned the teams, not the athletes who played
the game.

Naturally, Hulbert and the other founders characterized their action
as a moral one—a baseball reform movement. The new league's
constitution, after all, had been carefully drafted to keep the game
clean; it forbade Sunday games, as well as gambling and selling liquor at ballparks. In future years, team owners—Al Spalding the loudest among them
—would go on at great length about how the league had saved baseball from
gamblers, cheats, corruption and inefficiency.

The founding of the National League *was* undoubtedly a good thing for
baseball. The professional game couldn't have survived much longer under
the auspices of the NA. But to Hulbert and his colleagues, the reforms were
merely the means to a more important end: a stable, profitable business. The
National League protected its members from competition and gave the clubs
new powers over their labor pool—the players. In effect, the National
League set itself up as a self-regulating baseball monopoly, an infinitely more
efficient organization than the old, free-form National Association.

Even so, the National League was anything but an immediate success.
In its very first year, the Athletics and the Mutuals refused to make their final
western swings because they were losing money. Hulbert took a hard line
and expelled the two clubs, which represented two of the country's largest
cities, from the league. The next year, he expelled for life four Louisville
players for throwing games—gambling and cheating were proving to be hardy
foes. Teams came and went almost as quickly as they had under the National
Association—down to six in 1877; six again in 1878, but with three new

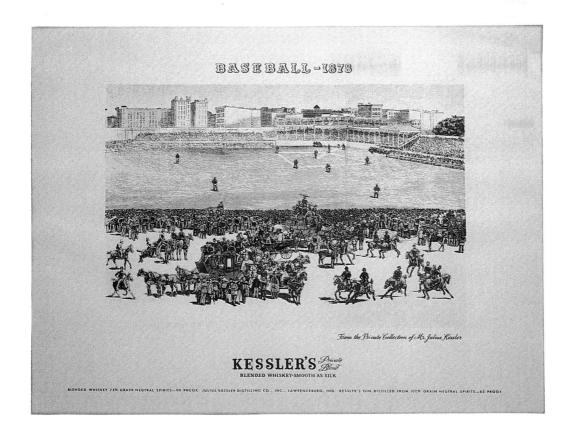

BASEBALL - 1878

From the Private Collection of Mr. Julius Kessler

KESSLER'S *Private Blend*
BLENDED WHISKEY-SMOOTH AS SILK

BLENDED WHISKEY 75% GRAIN NEUTRAL SPIRITS—90 PROOF. JULIUS KESSLER DISTILLING CO., INC., LAWRENCEBURG, IND. KESSLER'S GIN DISTILLED FROM 100% GRAIN NEUTRAL SPIRITS—85 PROOF.

cities; back to eight in 1879, but with four new cities. Most of them continued to lose money through the 1870s and on into the 1880s.

At the founding of the league, five directors were chosen by lot from among those representing the eight clubs. Because his was the first name picked out of the hat, Hartford's representative, insurance man Morgan Bulkeley, was named league president, an essentially ceremonial position. The league secretary, Nick Young, handled the day-to-day work, but Hulbert remained the real power in the game.

Hulbert, unfortunately, never lived to see his league solidly established and out of trouble. He fell ill early in 1882 and died in April at the age of 49. Ironically, one of his last great accomplishments was to include the infamous "reserve clause" in players' contracts that limited them to a particular team: this from the man who had stolen the Big Four from Boston and created his own league to escape the National Association's wrath.

Upon his death, Hulbert's league passed a resolution, stating "that to him alone is due the credit of having founded the National League, and to his able leadership, sound judgment and impartial management is the success of the league chiefly due." Nonetheless, William Hulbert was quickly forgotten. In the late 1930s the Baseball Hall of Fame wanted to honor a founder of the National League. Morgan Bulkeley of Hartford had been the National League's first president, so 60 years later it made sense to elect him to the hall. He is memorialized in bronze at Cooperstown—surely its least worthy member. William Hulbert, the man who conceived and created major league baseball, has yet to be honored with a plaque. ◑

Hulbert managed to keep liquor from being sold at NL games, but he couldn't stop the liquor business from cashing in on baseball's burgeoning popularity. Today baseball's top advertising beverage is beer; in 1878 it seemed to be blended whiskey.

The Elysian Fields, in Hoboken, New Jersey (following page), can lay claim to being baseball's first real home. Alexander Cartwright and his Knickerbockers rented the field and its dressing room for $75 for the 1846 season and, with their new rulebook in hand, lost their first home game, 23–1, to the New York Nine on June 19.

1870s Statistics

1871

National Association

	W	L	PCT	R	H	AVG
Philadelphia Athletics	22	7	.759	367	412	.310
Chicago White Stockings	20	9	.690	302	316	.253
Boston Red Stockings	22	10	.688	401	424	.295
Washington Olympics	16	15	.516	310	371	.265
Troy Haymakers	15	15	.500	353	370	.284
New York Mutuals	17	18	.486	302	392	.275
Cleveland Forest Citys	10	19	.345	249	326	.269
Fort Wayne Kekiongas	7	21	.250	137	179	.234
Rockford Forest Citys	6	21	.222	231	273	.253

League Leaders

Batting	L. Meyerle, PHI	.492
	C. McVey, BOS	.419
	S. King, TRO	.396
Runs	R. Barnes, BOS	66
	D. Birdsall, BOS	51
	J. Radcliff, PHI	47
	N. Cuthbert, PHI	47
Hits	R. Barnes, BOS	65
	C. McVey, BOS	65
	L. Meyerle, PHI	65
Wins	D. McBride, PHI	20
	A. Spalding, BOS	20
	G. Zettlein, CHI	18
Win Pct.	D. McBride, PHI	.800
	A. Spalding, BOS	.667
	G. Zettlein, CHI	.667

1872

National Association

	W	L	PCT	R	H	AVG
Boston Red Stockings	39	8	.830	521	671	.308
Philadelphia Athletics	30	14	.682	534	659	.298
Lord Baltimores	34	19	.642	597	717	.280
New York Mutuals	34	20	.630	523	681	.272
Troy Haymakers	15	10	.600	272	333	.297
Cleveland Forest Citys	6	15	.286	171	283	.296
Brooklyn Atlantics	8	27	.229	220	334	.230
Washington Olympics	2	7	.222	54	93	.250
Middletown Mansfields	5	19	.208	223	277	.273
Brooklyn Eckfords	3	26	.103	151	233	.206
Washington Nationals	0	11	.000	80	107	.238

League Leaders

Batting	D. Force, TRO/BAL	.412
	R. Barnes, BOS	.404
	A. Anson, PHI	.381
Runs	D. Eggler, NY	95
	G. Wright, BOS	86
	R. Barnes, BOS	81
Hits	D. Eggler, NY	102
	R. Barnes, BOS	97
	D. Force, TRO/BAL	93
Wins	A. Spalding, BOS	37
	C. Cummings, NY	33
	D. McBride, PHI	30
Win Pct.	A. Spalding, BOS	.822
	D. McBride, PHI	.682
	C. Cummings, NY	.623

1870s Statistics

1873

National Association

	W	L	PCT	R	H	AVG
Boston Red Stockings	43	16	.729	739	931	.323
Philadelphia White Stockings	36	17	.679	526	641	.265
Lord Baltimores	33	22	.600	624	783	.301
Philadelphia Athletics	28	23	.549	474	671	.281
New York Mutuals	29	24	.547	424	614	.267
Brooklyn Atlantics	17	37	.315	366	583	.252
Washington Nationals	8	31	.205	283	406	.249
Elizabeth Resolutes	2	21	.087	98	204	.221
Baltimore Marylands	0	5	.000	15	23	.136

League Leaders

Batting	R. Barnes, BOS	.402
	D. White, BOS	.382
	G. Wright, BOS	.378
Runs	R. Barnes, BOS	126
	G. Wright, BOS	98
	A. Spalding, BOS	85
Hits	R. Barnes, BOS	136
	G. Wright, BOS	126
	D. White, BOS	124
Wins	A. Spalding, BOS	41
	G. Zettlein, PHI (WS)	36
	B. Mathews, NY	29
Win Pct.	A. Spalding, BOS	.732
	G. Zettlein, PHI (WS)	.720
	C. Cummings, BAL (LB)	.667

1874

National Association

	W	L	PCT	R	H	AVG
Boston Red Stockings	52	18	.743	735	1033	.327
New York Mutuals	42	23	.646	500	708	.252
Philadelphia Athletics	33	23	.589	441	763	.331
Philadelphia White Stockings	29	29	.500	475	683	.269
Chicago White Stockings	28	31	.475	418	674	.263
Brooklyn Atlantics	22	33	.400	301	495	.222
Hartford Dark Blues	17	37	.315	371	611	.291
Lord Baltimores	9	38	.191	227	430	.228

League Leaders

Batting	J. McMullin, PHI (Ath)	.387
	C. McVey, BOS	.382
	S. Hastings, HAR	.371
Runs	C. McVey, BOS	90
	J. O'Rourke, BOS	80
	A. Spalding, BOS	80
Hits	C. McVey, BOS	131
	A. Spalding, BOS	121
	A. Leonard, BOS	119
Wins	A. Spalding, BOS	52
	B. Mathews, NY	42
	D. McBride, PHI (Ath)	33
Win Pct.	A. Spalding, BOS	.743
	B. Mathews, NY	.646
	D. McBride, PHI (Ath)	.600

1875

National Association

	W	L	PCT	R	H	AVG
Boston Red Stockings	71	8	.899	832	1161	.326
Philadelphia Athletics	53	20	.726	699	942	.286
Hartford Dark Blues	54	28	.659	554	863	.249
St. Louis Brown Stockings	39	29	.574	385	660	.249
Philadelphia White Stockings	37	31	.544	469	683	.258
Chicago White Stockings	30	37	.448	380	709	.250
New York Mutuals	30	38	.441	328	630	.227
St. Louis Red Stockings	4	14	.222	55	121	.181
New Haven Elm Citys	7	40	.149	170	368	.203
Washington Nationals	4	23	.148	96	181	.183
Philadelphia Centennials	2	12	.143	70	125	.228
Keokuk Westerns	1	12	.077	45	81	.167
Brooklyn Atlantics	2	42	.045	132	306	.192

League Leaders

Batting	R. Barnes, BOS	.372
	D. White, BOS	.355
	C. McVey, BOS	.352
Runs	R. Barnes, BOS	116
	G. Wright, BOS	105
	J. O'Rourke, BOS	96
Hits	R. Barnes, BOS	148
	C. McVey, BOS	138
	G. Wright, BOS	137
Wins	A. Spalding, BOS	57
	D. McBride, PHI (Ath)	44
	C. Cummings, HAR	35
Win Pct.	A. Spalding, BOS	.919
	D. McBride, PHI (Ath)	.759
	C. Cummings, HAR	.745

1870s Statistics

1876

National League

	W	L	PCT	GB	R	H	AVG
Chicago White Stockings	52	14	.788	—	624	926	.337
St. Louis Brown Stockings	45	19	.703	6	386	642	.259
Hartford Dark Blues	47	21	.691	6	429	711	.267
Boston Red Stockings	39	31	.557	15	471	723	.266
Louisville Grays	30	36	.455	22	280	641	.249
New York Mutuals	21	35	.375	26	260	494	.227
Philadelphia Athletics	14	45	.237	34½	378	646	.271
Cincinnati Red Stockings	9	56	.138	42½	238	555	.234

League Leaders

Batting	R. Barnes, CHI	.429
	G. Hall, PHI	.366
	A. Anson, CHI	.356
Runs	R. Barnes, CHI	126
	G. Wright, BOS	72
	J. Peters, CHI	70
Hits	R. Barnes, CHI	138
	J. Peters, CHI	111
	A. Anson, CHI	110
Wins	A. Spalding, CHI	47
	G. Bradley, StL	45
	T. Bond, HAR	31
Win Pct.	A. Spalding, CHI	.783
	J. Manning, BOS	.783
	T. Bond, HAR	.705

1877

National League

	W	L	PCT	GB	R	H	AVG
Boston Red Stockings	42	18	.700	—	419	700	.296
Louisville Grays	35	25	.583	7	339	659	.280
Hartford Dark Blues	31	27	.534	10	341	637	.270
St. Louis Brown Stockings	28	32	.467	14	284	531	.244
Chicago White Stockings	26	33	.441	15½	366	633	.278
Cincinnati Red Stockings	15	42	.263	25½	291	545	.255

League Leaders

Batting	D. White, BOS	.387
	J. Cassidy, HAR	.378
	C. McVey, CHI	.368
Runs	J. O'Rourke, BOS	68
	C. McVey, CHI	58
	G. Wright, BOS	58
Hits	D. White, BOS	103
	C. McVey, CHI	98
	J. O'Rourke, BOS	96
Wins	T. Bond, BOS	40
	J. Devlin, LOU	35
	T. Larkin, HAR	29
Win Pct.	T. Bond, BOS	.702
	J. Devlin, LOU	.583
	T. Larkin, HAR	.537

1870s Statistics

1878

National League

	W	L	PCT	GB	R	H	AVG
Boston Red Stockings	41	19	.683	—	298	535	.241
Cincinnati Red Stockings	37	23	.617	4	333	629	.276
Providence Grays	33	27	.550	8	353	604	.263
Chicago White Stockings	30	30	.500	11	371	677	.290
Indianapolis Hoosiers	24	36	.400	17	293	542	.236
Milwaukee Grays	15	45	.250	26	256	552	.250

League Leaders

Batting	P. Hines, PRO	.358
	A. Dalrymple, MIL	.354
	B. Ferguson, CHI	.351
Runs	D. Higham, PRO	60
	J. Start, CHI	58
	T. York, PRO	56
Hits	J. Start, CHI	100
	A. Dalrymple, MIL	96
	P. Hines, PRO	92
Wins	T. Bond, BOS	40
	W. White, CIN	30
	T. Larkin, CHI	29
Win Pct.	T. Bond, BOS	.678
	J. Ward, PRO	.629
	W. White, CIN	.588

1879

National League

	W	L	PCT	GB	R	H	AVG
Providence Grays	59	25	.702	—	612	1003	.296
Boston Red Stockings	54	30	.643	5	562	883	.274
Buffalo Bisons	46	32	.590	10	394	733	.252
Chicago White Stockings	46	33	.582	10½	437	808	.259
Cincinnati Red Stockings	43	37	.538	14	485	813	.264
Cleveland Blues	27	55	.329	31	322	666	.223
Syracuse Stars	22	48	.314	30	276	592	.227
Troy Trojans	19	56	.253	35½	321	673	.237

League Leaders

Batting	A. Anson, CHI	.396
	P. Hines, PRO	.357
	J. O'Rourke, PRO	.348
	M. Kelly, CIN	.348
Runs	C. Jones, BOS	85
	P. Hines, PRO	81
	G. Wright, PRO	79
Hits	P. Hines, PRO	146
	J. O'Rourke, PRO	126
	M. Kelly, CIN	120
Wins	J. Ward, PRO	47
	T. Bond, BOS	43
	W. White, CIN	43
Win Pct.	J. Ward, PRO	.734
	T. Bond, BOS	.694
	B. Mathews, PRO	.667

Town Ball Rules

The Rules & Regulations Governing The Game Of Base Ball As Adopted By
The Massachusetts Association Of Base Ball Players At Dedham, May 13, 1858,
as printed in "The Base Ball Player's Pocket Companion," Boston, Mayhew and Baker, 1859.

1. The Ball must weigh not less than two, nor more than two and three-quarter ounces, avoirdupois. It must measure not less than six and a half, nor more than eight and a half inches in circumference, and must be covered with leather.

2. The Bat must be round, and must not exceed two and a half inches in diameter in the thickest part. It must be made of wood, and may be of any length to suit the Striker.

3. Four Bases or Bounds shall constitute a round; the distance from each Base shall be sixty feet.

4. The Bases shall be wooden stakes, projecting four feet from the ground.

5. The Striker shall stand inside of a space of four feet in diameter, at equal distance between the first and fourth Bases.

6. The Thrower shall stand thirty-five feet from and on a parallel line with the Striker.

7. The Catcher shall not enter within the space occupied by the Striker, and must remain upon his feet in all cases while catching the Ball.

8. The Ball must be thrown—not pitched or tossed —to the Bat, on the side preferred by the Striker, and within reach of his Bat.

9. The Ball must be caught flying in all cases.

10. Players must take their knocks in the order in which they are numbered; and after the first innings is played, the turn will commence with the player succeeding the one who lost on the previous innings.

11. The Ball being struck at three times and missed, and caught each time by a player on the opposite side, the Striker shall be considered out. Or, if the Ball be ticked or knocked, and caught on the opposite side, the Striker shall be considered out. But if the Ball is not caught after being struck at three times, it shall be considered a knock, and the Striker obliged to run.

12. Should the Striker stand at the Bat without striking at good Balls thrown repeatedly at him, for the apparent purpose of delaying the game, or of giving advantage to players, the referees, after warning him, shall call one strike, and if he persists in such action, two and three strikes; when three strikes are called, he shall be subject to the same rules as if he struck at three fair Balls.

13. A player, having possession of the first Base, when the Ball is struck by the succeeding player, must vacate the Base, even at the risk of being put out; and when two players get on one Base, either by accident or otherwise, the player who arrived last is entitled to the base.

14. If a player, while running the Bases, be hit with the Ball thrown by one of the opposite side, before he has touched the home bound, while off a Base, he shall be considered out.

15. A player, after running the four Bases, on making the home bound, shall be entitled to one tally.

16. In playing all match games, when one is out, the side shall be considered out.

17. In playing all match games, one hundred tallies shall constitute the game, the making of which by either Club, that Club shall be judged the winner.

18. Not less than ten nor more than fourteen players from each Club, shall constitute a match in all games.

19. A person engaged on either side, shall not withdraw during the progress of the match, unless he be disabled, or by the consent of the opposite party.

20. The referees shall be chosen as follows: One from each Club, who shall agree upon a third man from some Club belonging to this Association, if possible. Their decision shall be final, and binding upon both parties.

21. The tallymen shall be chosen in the same manner as the referees.

Knickerbocker Rules

The Rules of The Knickerbocker Base Ball Club As Adopted September 23, 1845.

1. Members must strictly observe the time agreed upon for exercise, and be punctual in their attendance.

2. When assembled for exercise, the President, or in his absence the Vice-President, shall appoint an Umpire, who shall keep the game in a book provided for that purpose, and note all violations of the By-Laws and Rules during the time of exercise.

3. The presiding officer shall designate two members as Captains, who shall retire and make the match to be played, observing at the same time that the players put opposite to each other should be as nearly equal as possible; the choice of sides to be then tossed for, and the first in hand to be decided in like manner.

4. The bases shall be from "home" to second base, forty-two paces; from first to third base, forty-two paces, equidistant.

5. No stump match shall be played on a regular day of exercise.

6. If there should not be a sufficient number of members of the Club present at the time agreed upon to commence exercise, gentlemen not members may be chosen in to make up the match, which shall not be broken up to take in members that may afterwards appear; but, in all cases, members shall have the preference, when present, at the making of the match.

7. If members appear after the game is commenced they may be chosen in if mutually agreed upon.

8. The game to consist of twenty-one counts, or aces; but at the conclusion an equal number of hands must be played.

9. The ball must pitched, and not thrown, for the bat.

10. A ball knocked out the field, or outside the range of the first or third base, is foul.

11. Three balls being struck at and missed and the last one caught, is a hand out; if not caught is considered fair, and the striker bound to run.

12. If a ball be struck, or tipped, and caught, either flying or on the first bound, it is a hand out.

13. A player running the bases shall be out, if the ball is in the hands of an adversary on the base, or the runner is touched with it before he makes his base; it being understood, however, that in no instance is a ball to be thrown at him.

14. A player running who shall prevent an adversary from catching or getting the ball before making his base, is a hand out.

15. Three hands out, all out.

16. Players must take their strike in regular turn.

17. All disputes and differences relative to the game, to be decided by the Umpire, from which there is no appeal.

18. No ace or base can be made on a foul strike.

19. A runner cannot be put out in making one base, when a balk is made by the pitcher.

20. But one base allowed when a ball bounds out of the field when struck.

Courtesy Tom Heitz, National Baseball Library, Cooperstown, NY.

INDEX

FOR FURTHER READING

Melvin A. Adelman, *A Sporting Time,*
University of Illinois Press, 1986.

Warren Goldstein, *Playing for Keeps: A
History of Early Baseball,* Cornell
University Press, 1989.

Robert W. Henderson, *Ball, Bat and
Bishop,* Rockport Press, 1947.

Irving A. Leitner, *Baseball: Diamond in
the Rough,* Criterion, 1972.

Harold Seymour, *Baseball: The Early
Years,* Oxford University Press, 1960.

David Q. Voigt, *American Baseball:
From Gentleman's Sport to the
Commissioner System,* University of
Oklahoma Press, 1966.

PICTURE CREDITS

Front Cover: The Harvard Base Ball Team courtesy of the Harvard University Archives.

Back Cover: John Lowell circa 1866, Lowells of Boston Base Ball Club, from the collection of Mark Rucker.

Our Game
4-5 Anthony Neste; 6-7 International Museum of Photography at George Eastman House, Rochester, New York.

Common Ancestors
8-9 Mark Rucker; 10 The Bettmann Archive; 11 (top) Bodleian Library, Oxford, England; 11 (bottom) National Institute of Anthropology and History, S.E.P., Mexico City, Mexico; 12 Mark Rucker; 13 Neil Leifer; 14 The Connecticut Historical Society, Hartford, Connecticut; 15 Mark Rucker; 16 Janice E. Rettaliata; 17 Thomas Carwile Collection/Renée Comet Photography; 18-19 Library of Congress and John Thorn.

The Doubleday Myth
24-25 Dennis Goldstein Collection; 26 Library of Congress; 27 Dennis Goldstein Collection; 28 (left) Brown Brothers; 28 (right) Spalding Collection, Miriam and Ira D. Wallach Division of Art, Prints and Photographs, New York Public Library, Astor, Lenox and Tilden Foundations; 29 (left) The Lester S. Levy Sheet Music Collection, Johns Hopkins University; 29 (right) Michael Olenick Collection; 30 (left) Mark Rucker; 30 (right) Lew Lipset; 31 Library of Congress; 32 Bettmann Newsphotos; 33 (left) Janice E. Rettaliata; 33 (right) Mark Rucker; 34 Boston Public Library courtesy of the National Baseball Library, Cooperstown, New York; 35 American Antiquarian Society; 36 (left) R. M. Parfitt; 36 (right) Peter Tarry/Action-Plus; 37 (left) Library of Congress; 37 (right) Spalding Collection, Miriam and Ira D. Wallach Division of Art, Prints and Photographs, New York Public Library, Astor, Lenox and Tilden Foundations; 38-39 Mark Rucker; 40 Thomas Carwile Collection/ Renée Comet Photography; 41 (left) Brown Brothers; 41 (right) Mark Rucker; 42-43 National Baseball Library, Cooperstown, New York; 43 Culver Pictures.

The New York Game
44-45 I. N. Phelps Stokes Collection, Miriam and Ira D. Wallach Division of Art, Prints and Photographs, New York Public Library, Astor, Lenox and Tilden Foundations; 46 (top) National Baseball Library, Cooperstown, New York; 46 (bottom) Mark Rucker; 47 Spalding Collection, Miriam and Ira D. Wallach Division of Art, Prints and Photographs, New York Public Library, Astor, Lenox and Tilden Foundations; 48-49 Spalding Collection, Miriam and Ira D. Wallach Division of Art, Prints and Photographs, New York Public Library, Astor, Lenox and Tilden Foundations; 49 Dennis Goldstein Collection; 50 © 1990 The Gifted Line, John Grossman, Inc., from the John Grossman Collection of Antique Images; 51 Dennis Goldstein Collection; 52 John Thorn; 53 Ron Menchine Collection/Renée Comet Photography; 54 (left) Maryland Historical Society; 54 (right) Library of Congress; 55 National Baseball Library, Cooperstown, New York; 56 Mark Rucker; 57 Mark Rucker; 58 (left) National Baseball Library, Cooperstown, New York; 58-59 Culver Pictures; 59 (right) Dennis Goldstein Collection.

For Health and Recreation
60 Thomas Carwile Collection/Renée Comet Photography; 61 National Baseball Library, Cooperstown, New York; 62 (both) Mark Rucker; 63 Thomas Carwile Collection/Renée Comet Photography; 64 (left) Mark Rucker; 64 (right) Brown Brothers; 65 (top) New York Public Library; 65 (bottom) Mark Rucker; 66 (both) Mark Rucker; 67 Dennis Goldstein; 68 National Baseball Library, Cooperstown, New York; 69 (top) Dennis Goldstein Collection; 69 (bottom) Mark Rucker; 70-71 National Baseball Library, Cooperstown, New York/Baseball Ink; 71 Boston Public Library; 72 Ron Menchine Collection/Renée Comet Photography; 73 (top) courtesy Harvard University Archives; 73 (center) Spalding Collection, Miriam and Ira D. Wallach Division of Art, Prints and Photographs, New York Public Library, Astor, Lenox and Tilden Foundations; 73 (bottom) Mark Rucker; 74 courtesy Harvard University Archives; 74-75 courtesy Harvard University Archives; 75 Dennis Goldstein Collection; 76 Mark Rucker; 77 Library of Congress; 78 Ron Menchine Collection/Renée Comet Photography; 79 National Baseball Library, Cooperstown, New York; 80 Mark Rucker; 81 Mark Rucker.

The Wright Brothers
82 *The Sporting News;* 83 Ron Menchine Collection/Renée Comet Photography; 84 Mark Rucker; 85 Barry Sloate; 87 (top) Mark Rucker; 87 (bottom) Ron Menchine Collection/Renée Comet Photography; 88 The Lester S. Levy Sheet Music Collection, Johns Hopkins University; 89 Mark Rucker; 90 Mark Rucker; 91 Thomas Carwile Collection/ Renée Comet Photography; 92 (both) Spalding Collection, Miriam and Ira D. Wallach Division of Art, Prints and Photographs, New York Public Library, Astor, Lenox and Tilden Foundations; 93 Mark Rucker; 94 (left) Spalding Collection, Miriam and Ira D. Wallach Division of Art, Prints and Photographs, New York Public Library, Astor, Lenox and Tilden Foundations; 94 (right) Mark Rucker; 95 Mark Rucker; 96-97 Mark Rucker; 97 Mark Rucker; 98 Mark Rucker; 99 Thomas Carwile Collection/ Renée Comet Photography.

Growing Pains
100-101 Museum of Art, Rhode Island School of Design, Jesse Metcalf and Walter H. Kimball Funds, Providence, Rhode Island; 102 Dennis Goldstein Collection; 103 Barry Sloate; 105 (top) The Bettmann Archive; 105 (bottom) National Baseball Library, Cooperstown, New York; 106 Mark Rucker; 107 (left) Mark Rucker; 107 (right) Mark Rucker; 108 Ron Menchine Collection/Renée Comet Photography; 109 (left) Brown Brothers; 109 (right) Mark Rucker; 110 (left) Thomas Carwile Collection/Renée Comet Photography; 110 (right) Mark Rucker; 111 Mark Rucker; 112 Lew Lipset; 113 Northeastern University courtesy Boston Public Library; 114 Mark Rucker; 115 National Baseball Library, Cooperstown, New York.

Father Chadwick
116-117 Mark Rucker; 118 (left) Mark Rucker; 118 (right) Culver Pictures; 119 Spalding Collection, Miriam and Ira D. Wallach Division of Art, Prints and Photographs, New York Public Library, Astor, Lenox and Tilden Foundations; 120 (left) Dennis Goldstein Collection; 120 (right) Ron Menchine Collection/ Renée Comet Photography; 121 National Baseball Library, Cooperstown, New York; 122 Thomas Carwile Collection/ Renée Comet Photography; 124 Mark Rucker; 125 (left) The Lester S. Levy Sheet Music Collection, Johns Hopkins University; 125 (right) Smithsonian Institution; 126-127 The Connecticut Historical Society, Hartford, Connecticut; 128 (left) The Lester S. Levy Sheet Music Collection, Johns Hopkins University; 128 (right) Thomas Carwile Collection/Renée Comet Photography; 129 Ron Menchine Collection/Renée

Comet Photography; 130 Dennis Goldstein Collection; 131 (top) National Baseball Library, Cooperstown, New York; 131 (bottom) Ron Menchine Collection/Renée Comet Photography; 132 John Thorn; 133 (left) Ron Menchine Collection/Renée Comet Photography; 133 (right) Ron Menchine Collection/ Renée Comet Photography.

Diamond Dust
134 Smithsonian Institution; 135 Thomas Carwile Collection/Renée Comet Photography; 136 Ron Menchine Collection/Renée Comet Photography; 137 © 1990 The Gifted Line, John Grossman, Inc., from the John Grossman Collection of Antique Images; 138 Ron Vesely; 139 (left) Mark Rucker; 139 (right) National Baseball Library, Cooperstown, New York, courtesy of Mark Rucker; 140 Spalding Collection, Miriam and Ira D. Wallach Division of Art, Prints and Photographs, New York Public Library, Astor, Lenox and Tilden Foundations; 141 Mark Rucker; 142 Mark Rucker; 142-143 The Bettmann Archive; 144 Ron Menchine Collection/ Renée Comet Photography; 145 (left) Mark Rucker; 145 (right) Adrian Murrell/Allsport; 146 (top left) Library of Congress courtesy of Mark Rucker; 146 (top right) Mark Rucker; 146 (bottom) Thomas Carwile Collection/Renée Comet Photography; 147 (top left) Mark Rucker; 147 (top center) Dennis Goldstein Collection; 147 (bats, left to right) National Baseball Library, Cooperstown, New York; Dennis Goldstein Collection; Thomas Carwile Collection/Renée Comet Photography; 147 (bottom left) Thomas Carwile Collection/Renée Comet Photography; 147 (bottom center) Thomas Carwile Collection/Renée Comet Photography; 147 (center) John Thorn; 150 (left) Dennis Goldstein Collection; 150 (right) Thomas Carwile Collection/Renée Comet Photography; 151 Doug Hoke/ *Sports Illustrated;* 152 National Baseball Library, Cooperstown, New York; 153 Mark Rucker.

The Great Tour
154-155 courtesy of the New-York Historical Society; 156 Mark Rucker; 157 (left) Mark Rucker; 157 (right) Culver Pictures; 158-159 (all) Thomas Carwile Collection/Renée Comet Photography; 160 (left) Mark Rucker; 160 (right) Lew Lipset; 161 courtesy of the New-York Historical Society; 162 National Baseball Library, Cooperstown, New York; 162-163 Thomas Carwile Collection/ Renée Comet Photography; 163 The Pennsylvania Historical Society; 164

(left) Mark Rucker; 164-165 Spalding Collection, Miriam and Ira D. Wallach Division of Art, Prints and Photographs, New York Public Library, Astor, Lenox and Tilden Foundations; 165 Mark Rucker; 166 Mark Rucker; 167 Dennis Goldstein Collection; 168 Mark Rucker; 169 Spalding Collection, Miriam and Ira D. Wallach Division of Art, Prints and Photographs, The New York Public Library, Astor, Lenox and Tilden Foundations.

A Major Undertaking
170 Library of Congress; 171 Ron Menchine Collection/Renée Comet Photography; 172 (left) Culver Pictures; 172 (right) Thomas Carwile Collection/ Renée Comet Photography; 173 (both) Mark Rucker; 174 Spalding Collection, Miriam and Ira D. Wallach Division of Art, Prints and Photographs, New York Public Library, Astor, Lenox and Tilden Foundations; 175 Chicago Historical Society; 176 (left) Maryland Historical Society; 176 (right) Mark Rucker; 178 Thomas Carwile Collection/Renée Comet Photography; 179 (left) Mark Rucker; 179 (right) Thomas Carwile Collection/ Renée Comet Photography; 180-181 courtesy Yale University Art Gallery, Whitney Collection of Sporting Art, New Haven, Connecticut; 182 Thomas Carwile Collection/Renée Comet Photography; 184 Thomas Carwile Collection/Renée Comet Photography; 185 Thomas Carwile Collection/Renée Comet Photography.

ACKNOWLEDGMENTS

The author and editors wish to thank:

Peter P. Clark, Tom Heitz, Bill Deane, Patricia Kelly, Dan Bennett, Frank Rollins and the staffs of the National Baseball Hall of Fame and National Baseball Library, Cooperstown, New York; Helen Bowie Campbell and Gregory J. Schwalenberg, Babe Ruth Museum, Baltimore, Maryland; Ellen Hughes, National Museum of American History, Smithsonian Institution, Washington, D.C.; George Hobart and Mary Ison, Prints and Photographs Division, Library of Congress, Washington, D.C.; Venessa Whinney, London, England; Marcy Silver, The Historical Society of Pennsylvania, Philadelphia, Pennsylvania; Dennis Goldstein, Atlanta, Georgia; Thomas and Kay Carwile, Petersburg, Virginia; John Thorn and Richard Puff of Baseball Ink, Saugerties, New York; Barry Sloate, Brooklyn, New York; Clarence "Lefty" Blasco, Van Nuys, California; Bob Davids, Washington, D.C.; Adrienne Aurichio, New York, New York; Lillian Clark, Cleveland Public Library, Cleveland, Ohio; Deborah Cohen, *LIFE* Picture Service, New York, New York; Renée Comet, Renée Comet Photography, Washington, D.C.; Sarah Antonecchia, UPI/Bettmann Newsphotos, New York, New York; Mrs. Meredith Collins, Brown Brothers, Sterling, Pennsylvania; Tom Logan, Culver Pictures, New York, New York; Stephen P. Gietschier, *The Sporting News,* St. Louis, Missouri; Karen Carpenter and Sunny Smith, *Sports Illustrated,* New York, New York; Nat Andriani, AP/Wide World Photos, New York, New York; Joe Borras, Accokeek, Maryland; Dave Kelly, Library of Congress, Washington, D.C.; Wade and Nick Capetta, Alexandria, Virginia; Nick Spencer, Washington, D.C.; Bruce L. Prentice, The Canadian Baseball Hall of Fame, Toronto, Ontario, Canada; Robert L. Tiemann, St. Louis, Missouri; Robert F. Bluthardt, San Angelo, Texas; Wayne Martin, Atlanta, Georgia; Candice Cochrane, Charlestown, Massachusetts; Jayne E. Rohrich, Alexandria, Virginia; Francisco Montellano, Pablo Labastida, Mexico City, Mexico.

Illustrations: 20–21, 22–23, 52, 86, 104, 148–149, 177 by Sam Ward.

World of Baseball is produced and
published by Redefinition, Inc.

WORLD OF BASEBALL

Editor	Glen B. Ruh
Design Director	Robert Barkin
Production Director	Irv Garfield
Senior Writer	Jonathan Kronstadt
Features Editor	Sharon Cygan
Text Editor	Carol Gardner
Staff Writer	Mark Lazen
Picture Editors	Rebecca Hirsh
	Louis P. Plummer
Design	Edwina Smith
	Sue Pratt
	Collette Conconi
	Monique Strawderman
Copy Preparation	Anthony K. Pordes
	Ronald Stanley
	Kimberly Fornshill Holmlund
Editorial Research	Janet Pooley
	Ed Dixon
	Denise Meringolo
Index	Lee McKee

REDEFINITION

Administration	Margaret M. Higgins
	June M. Nolan
Fulfillment Manager	Karen DeLisser
Marketing Director	Wayne B. Butler
Finance Director	Vaughn A. Meglan
PRESIDENT	Edward Brash

Library of Congress Cataloging-in-Publication Data
The old ball game/Mark Alvarez.
  (World of Baseball)
Includes index.
  1. Baseball—United States—History.
  2. Baseball players—United States— Biography.
I. Title. II. Series.
GV863.A1A47 1990   90–38508
796.357'0973—dc20
ISBN 0–924588–09–8

Printed in the U.S.A.
10 9 8 7 6 5 4 3 2 1

CONTRIBUTORS

Mark Alvarez is a free-lance writer on baseball and other important subjects. He has been an associate editor of *The National Pastime* for the Society of American Baseball Research, a contributing editor to *Sports Heritage* and the author of *The Official Baseball Hall of Fame Answer Book*. As a teenager in Connecticut, he was an all-star infielder before taking two state high-school championships in the two-mile run.

Henry Staat is Series Consultant for World of Baseball. A member of the Society for American Baseball Research since 1982, he helped initiate the concept for the series. He is an editor with Wadsworth, Inc., a publisher of college textbooks.

Mark Rucker is a free-lance artist and a collector of baseball pictures, many of which appear in this book. He is picture editor and co-author of a number of books, including *The Babe: A Life in Pictures* and *The Ballplayers*. An avid fan of 19th-century baseball, he uses his personal time machine to gather images and to visit his favorite Victorian ballparks.

The editors also wish to thank the following writers for their contributions to this book: Randy Rieland, Washington, D.C.; Gerald Jonas, New York, NY; David Rice, Washington, D.C.; Rob Kiener, Washington, D.C.; John Ross, Washington, D.C.

This book is one of a series that celebrates America's national pastime.

Redefinition also offers World of Baseball Top Ten Stat Finders.

For subscription information and prices, write:
  Customer Service, Redefinition Inc.
  P.O. Box 25336
  Alexandria, Virginia 22313

The text of this book is set in Century Old Style; display type is Helvetica and Gill Sans. The paper is 70 pound Warrenflo Gloss supplied by Stanford Paper Company. Typesetting by Intergraphics, Inc., Alexandria, Virginia. Color separation by Lanman Progressive, Washington, D.C. Printed and bound by Ringier America, New Berlin, Wisconsin.